THE L.A.

L.A. SUPERLATIVES is
Los Angeles—the w
sports figures and the
former head writer of "The Tonight Show" and
writer/ producer of such successful television series
as "Alice" and "Fish," covers the city from top to
bottom, and from the inside out. It's fun, it's
fascinating, it's L.A. at its best!

★   ★   ★   ★   ★   ★   ★

Answers to the questions on the back cover:
1. Marilyn Monroe's. **2.** Mrs./Mr. John/Jeanne Moray of Englewood. **3.** Pirates of the Caribbean.
4. Mrs. Marvin Davis, with over one billion dollars in assets. **5.** The "Ocean House" built by William Randolph Hearst in Santa Monica for girlfriend Marion Davies, it included 37 fireplaces and 55 bathrooms. **6.** Judy Garland, Hedy Lamarr, Veronica Lake, and Louise Lasser were all accused of shoplifting. **7.** $225,000—Alan Alda's pay per episode of M*A*S*H. **8.** Kenneth Bianchi, "The Hillside Strangler," who with his cousin's assistance killed at least five women in 1977 and 1978. **9.** $20.5 million.
10. Autoerotica asphyxia, which accounts for 20 to 30 deaths every year in L.A. County.

L.A.
SUPERLATIVES

ATTENTION: SCHOOLS AND CORPORATIONS

WARNER books are available at quantity discounts with bulk purchase for educational, business, or sales promotional use. For information, please write to: SPECIAL SALES DEPARTMENT, WARNER BOOKS, 666 FIFTH AVENUE, NEW YORK, N.Y. 10103.

**ARE THERE WARNER BOOKS
YOU WANT BUT CANNOT FIND IN YOUR LOCAL STORES?**

You can get any WARNER BOOKS title in print. Simply send title and retail price, plus 50c per order and 50c per copy to cover mailing and handling costs for each book desired. New York State and California residents add applicable sales tax. Enclose check or money order only, no cash please, to: WARNER BOOKS, P.O. BOX 690, NEW YORK, N.Y. 10019.

L.A. Superlatives

BY ROY KAMMERMAN

WARNER BOOKS

A Warner Communications Company

WARNER BOOKS EDITION

Copyright © 1987 by Roy Kammerman
All rights reserved.

Cover design by Carmine Vecchio

Warner Books, Inc.
666 Fifth Avenue
New York, N.Y. 10103

A Warner Communications Company

Printed in the United States of America

First Printing: August, 1987

10 9 8 7 6 5 4 3 2 1

This book is for Bino, Mark, Alice,
Boni, On, Adam, Jane and Ken.
Each a true superlative.

ACKNOWLEDGMENTS

L.A. Superlatives would have been impossible without the cooperation of a whole city-full of people.

Particularly deserving of thanks are officer Margie Reid, press relations officer of the office of Chief of Police of the Los Angeles Police Department and officer Howard Rudoff of the LAPD Public Affairs Section.

I am in debt to Hal Harkness, director of Interscholastic Athletics, Los Angeles Unified School District, and to the press information departments of the Los Angeles Dodgers, Angels, Rams, Raiders, Lakers, and Clippers, as well as to the press information departments of UCLA and USC.

The Greater Los Angeles Visitors and Convention Bureau deserves our gratitude as does the Beverly Hills Chamber of Commerce. The Los Angeles Library and the *Los Angeles Times* were of inestimable help.

I enjoy having this opportunity to thank those who helped with research, first of whom is Soni Bayles, a fine free-lance writer, whose relationship to this book is nothing less than surrogate mother. Gabrielle Johnston of the television show "Family Feud" charmed many a bird off many a tree in pursuit of closely held truths. My longtime friend, Bonnie Young, helped me with this project as she has with so many others. Debi Taub contributed handsomely to this book.

A special thanks is due to Dan Douma and Gabriella Zinke and Monica, Carolyn, Hugh and Yolanda of the Writer's Computer Store who took the dumbest kid in the class and with supernatural patience taught me, byte by byte, how to use the word processor.

Finally, attention must be paid to Jim Frost, my editor, who had the courage to taste a sample and order the whole, and whose enthusiasm, guidance and never-ending flow of kindnesses made this book not only possible, but fun.

Together, we have, I believe, created something of value to Los Angeles. As we hopefully extend this book to a series, to include *New York Superlatives*, *Chicago Superlatives* and other cities around the world, I hope I am lucky enough to have such talented and enthusiastic collaborators.

AUTHOR'S NOTE

The facts in this book are, to the best of my knowledge, correct. Some things, such as "Highest Point In The City," remain eternal (I hope the developers don't take this as a challenge), but the accuracy of much of our data is at the mercy of the ambition and caprice of millions of hyperkinetic Los Angelenos who daily set new records in the sublime and in the ridiculous.

If you find a fact that has been usurped by a new statistic or if we have omitted a superlative which you feel belongs in this book—and there must be hundreds—please write us. If we can authenticate it, we will make every effort to include your name as a contributor in our next edition.

If you yourself have achieved a Los Angeles record of any sort, or are going to try for one, notify us so we can verify it for possible inclusion in our next *L.A. Superlatives*.

Write to: L.A. Superlatives, Suite 1, 704 N. Gardner, Los Angeles, CA. 90046 or Warner Books, 666 Fifth Avenue, New York, N.Y. 10103.

TABLE OF CONTENTS

Foreword: Los Angeles!	xiii
Entertainment	1
The People	35
Health	85
Nature	101
Crime	119
The City	155
Sports and Personal Achievements	199

LOS ANGELES!

The geography of what, in this book, we call Los Angeles meanders. Sometimes we are talking about Los Angeles the city with its specific political boundaries. But other times we include its playgrounds and bedrooms: Beverly Hills and Malibu, Palm Springs, Newport, Santa Barbara, and the new city of West Hollywood. To separate them from Los Angeles is to separate the Vatican from Rome. Does any visitor think Los Angeles and fail to contemplate Disneyland? When Los Angelenos play on the beaches of Malibu or the sands of Palm Springs, are they aware of being on alien territory, or do they feel they have, in fact, never left home? So we, like the visitor or the true Los Angeleno, have chosen to wander freely, but we will always keep you fully informed just where you are.

★
Entertainment

★

LOS ANGELES, world's greatest exporter of entertainment, is itself a magnet for those who have heard the legends, have tasted the products, and want to see how it's all done. Forty percent of all visitors come to play.

The visions projected by Hollywood, always in superlatives, are found by visitors, astonishingly enough, to have basis in fact. Here are a few of the facts, genuine superlatives, separated from the enchanting myths.

THE STAR'S HOME TOURISTS WANT MOST TO SEE

Although her attempt at a new program in 1986 was met by indifference and went off the air almost immediately, the star whose home Hollywood visitors most want to see, according to tour guides, is that of Lucille Ball.

The next most requested home is that of Robert Wagner and Natalie Wood, prompted apparently by interest in her bizarre death by drowning from her yacht.

Barbra Streisand's home is third, followed by that of Jimmy Stewart and a tie between old-timers Milton Berle and George Burns.

WEALTHIEST WOMAN IN SHOW BIZ

The wealthiest woman in show business in the Los Angeles area is probably Mrs. John Lennon (L.A. is a part-time home) with assets of $200 million plus.

Second: Pia Zadora, $200 million, but probably without the plus.

ONLY AMUSEMENT PARK BANNED TO RUSSIANS

The only amusement park in the world which is forbidden to visiting Soviet diplomats and journalists is Disneyland. The Magic Kingdom lies in a part of the L.A. metropolitan area that has been declared off-limits by our State Department to these particular members of the Soviet Union. Private Soviet citizens may, however, explore the mysteries of Space Mountain and Fantasyland as they desire.

ANIMAL MOST EMPLOYED IN MOVIES AND TV

The animal seen more than any other in movies and TV shows produced in Hollywood is the dog.

Runners-up: horses, house cats, chimps, lions, tigers, seals.

HIGHEST ANIMAL RENTAL

The most expensive animal you can rent in Los Angeles is a grizzly bear at $1,000 a day. Other top animal rentals:

Elephant	$500 to $1,000
Lion or tiger	$600
Black Bear	$400
Chimp	$400
Seal	$400
Dog	$150 to $400
Cat	$200
Wolf	$200
Fox	$150

Animals (even dogs and cats) working in TV or movies must be accompanied by a trainer who is a member of local 399, a branch of the Teamsters Union. They charge $17.29 an hour for accompanying domestic animals and $20.65 for wild animals.

Animals are protected by the American Humane Society, which sends trained observers at its own expense to watch over animals on movie and TV sets.

RONALD REAGAN'S LAST FILM

The last film Ronald Reagan made was *The Killers* in 1964 when he was 52 years old. The picture was made for television but was judged too violent for home consumption and exhibited only in theaters.

MOST EXOTIC ANIMALS OWNED BY A STAR

The largest collection of unusual animals owned by any one show-business personality is the collection of singer

Michael Jackson. In 1986 Michael's giraffe was taken into custody by state fish and game authorities who claimed that it was imported illegally and was being improperly housed. Michael brought everything up to code, and he and his giraffe are together again.

MOST VISITED STAR'S GRAVE

The most visited star's grave is that of Marilyn Monroe in the Corridor of Memories in Westwood Memorial Cemetery. She is buried in a plain crypt which says simply, "Marilyn Monroe, 1926–1962." Marilyn's ex-husband, Joe DiMaggio, had six red roses placed on her crypt three times a week for twenty years.

HIGHEST PAID MAN IN THE UNITED STATES

Only once in Hollywood history has a movie executive been the highest-paid man in the United States. In 1927 Louis B. Mayer of MGM with a salary of $1,296,000 was the most generously compensated executive in the United States.

THE MOST POPULAR RIDE AT DISNEYLAND

The most popular attraction at Disneyland is the Pirates of the Caribbean.

Second is Space Mountain, followed by: Haunted Mansion, It's A Small World, Big Thunder Mountain Railroad, Matterhorn Bobsled.

MOST POPULAR SOUVENIR AT DISNEYLAND

The most popular souvenir sold at Disneyland is the Mickey Mouse ears, which sell at the rate of 10,000 pairs a week.

HIGHEST ALTITUDE ACHIEVED BY MAN FLYING A LAWN CHAIR

The highest altitude ever achieved in free flight by a man in a lawn chair was attained in 1982 by Larry Walters of Los Angeles, who piloted a standard, unmodified Sears lawn chair to a height of three miles.

The craft was held aloft by 24 helium-filled weather balloons attached to the lawn chair with three nylon ropes. With no previous flight experience of any kind, Walters took off from his fiancée's backyard in Redondo Beach.

The lawn chair rose swiftly, flawlessly, but was soon much too high. Euphoric, Walters was unaware of his danger until he suddenly saw a jumbo jet almost collision close and became aware of a numbing cold. He made the return to earth by puncturing the balloons with a pellet gun. Finally he skimmed across a roof in Long Beach and crash-landed his metal chair and balloons in the power lines above the city streets. Miraculously he was unscratched. He could easily have been the toast of Long Beach.

Since he first saw the balloon man at Disneyland at age 7, Walters had dreamed of riding the heavens supported only by a clutch of balloons. His flight, quixotic as it seemed, was the result of 20 years of dreaming and planning.

BIGGEST DAY AT DISNEYLAND

Although Disneyland keeps attendance figures secret, the largest gate in the park's history was on August 16, 1969. The occasion: the opening of the Haunted Mansion.

Universal Tours had its biggest day July 5, 1986, with 31,000 visitors.

MOST POPULAR TOURIST ATTRACTION

The most popular tourist attraction in the Los Angeles area is not Disneyland; it's Beverly Hills. Second is Hollywood. (Although exact figures are not available, tourist surveys show that these are the two top-priority tourist destinations.) Disneyland is third, followed by Universal Tours. Fourth is the Spruce Goose (Howard Hughes' flying boat) and the Queen Mary. Fifth: Knotts Berry Farm.

MOST DANGEROUS CURVE IN LOS ANGELES

The most dangerous curve in Los Angeles was on Sunset Boulevard; for years it brought stunned motorists to a screeching halt. As they approached the curve, they saw a house with a large white garage door on which a famous comedian used to project porno movies from his Hollywood Hills hideout. Even the sign Dangerous Curves Ahead did nothing to prepare drivers for what they saw, and the spot became known as Dead Man's Curve. The stunt is attributed to comedian Red Skelton.

HIGHEST GROSSING MOVIE

Gone With the Wind, in 1986 dollars, is the highest-grossing film of all time. Domestic sales alone have totaled more than $321,603,000.

MOST POPULAR RADIO STATION

The most listened-to radio station in Los Angeles is KPWR-FM (105.9), known popularly as POWER 106, with 1.4 million listeners a week.

A controversy surrounds the type of music this most successful of all stations plays. The station, according to its management, plays "contemporary hit radio" or a top-40 format. Billboard chart-makers, who don't even include KPWR in making up their charts, claim the station plays "urban/contemporary" or black music for black listeners, but doesn't wish to be so labeled. According to Arbitron ratings, only 18 percent of KPWR's listeners are black.

MOST LISTENED-TO TALK RADIO

The most listened-to radio station with an all-talk format is KABC-AM (790), which ranks third among all stations in Los Angeles.

LONGEST TIME IN ONE APARTMENT

Mae West is believed to hold the record, at least for Hollywood stars, for the longest tenancy in the same apartment. She lived in the same white-on-white apartment in Ravenswood Apartments from 1932 until she died in 1980, a total of 48 years.

MOST HOMES LIVED IN BY ONE STAR

No star, peripatetic as many are, has even approached the number of homes occupied in Los Angeles by Judy Garland, who in 40 years and two marriages, lived in 25 different places, sometimes two or three different addresses in a year.

Her dwellings included small unfurnished apartments to her mother's house and rented mansions. For a brief period she rented Mary Martin's house. Outside Los Angeles, "home" was an equally impressive array of hotels, houses, and apartments in other cities.

STUNTMAN HOLDING THE MOST RECORDS

No stuntman in history has held as many stunt records as Dar Allen Robinson:

Highest fall while on fire: 190 feet

Highest fall from a building onto an air bag: 311 feet (31 stories)

Highest fee ever paid a stuntman: $100,000. For the movie *High Point* he jumped from a 1,100-foot-high tower, opening his parachute 300 feet from the ground.

Longest car jump from ramp to surface: The world's record for leaping a car from ramp to surface is 179 feet, 29 feet farther than the Wright Brothers first flight.

Highest movie dive from a helicopter: 286 feet (almost 29 stories) onto an air bag in Buena Park, September, 1980. A stuntman who held the previous record of 280 feet died trying to regain his title when the air bag he dove onto collapsed. Robinson himself was killed in 1986 in a routine stunt when his motorcycle ran off an embankment and he became impaled on a sagebrush branch.

HIGHEST PRICE FOR SCREEN RIGHTS TO A NOVEL

The most money ever paid by Hollywood for the rights to a novel was $3.5 million to William P. Blatty for *The Exorcist*.

LARGEST THEATER CURTAIN

The largest theater curtain in Los Angeles is located in a cemetery. It is used to present the world's largest religious painting, Jan Styka's *Crucifixion*, which is 45 feet high and 190 feet long, and its companion painting *Resurrection* by Robert Clark, which is half its size. Framed by the world's largest curtain, they are located in the Hall of Crucifixion at Forest Lawn Cemetery in Glendale.

LARGEST TV SYNDICATOR

MCA is television's largest syndicator, with 8,562 episodes of 140 series.

MOST MARRIED ACTORS

Artie Shaw ties with Mickey Rooney for the title of most married actor. Each married eight times.

Stan Laurel was also married eight times, but his marriages involved only four women, two of whom he married three times each—probably some other kind of record.

MOST MARRIED ACTRESSES

Beauty apparently isn't a big factor in ensuring a happy marriage. Two of Hollywood's most beautiful women are tied for the title of most married actress. They are Elizabeth Taylor and Lana Turner, each with seven trips to the altar.

LARGEST YACHT OWNED BY A MOVIE STAR

The largest yacht owned by a movie star is that of singer-host John Davidson whose *Principia*, berthed at Marina del Rey, is a beautifully maintained classic 90-foot motor yacht that dwarfs all but a handful of boats at the Marina. Davidson occasionally charters it out to make ends meet.

Other star-owned yachts: Robert Goulet's *Rogo*, a 60-foot Pace Maker motor boat. Sylvester Stallone is the captain of a 47-foot sailboat. Buddy Ebsen designed from scratch a catamaran called *Polynesian Concept* that is so

FIRST OSCAR CEREMONIES

The first Academy Awards ceremony was held in the Hotel Hollywood Roosevelt in 1929.

LARGEST OUTDOOR MOVIE SET

The largest outdoor movie set in Hollywood history was that for the silent movie *Intolerance* directed by D.W. Griffith in 1916.

HIGHEST-PAID MOVIE EXEC

By far the highest-paid movie executive in Hollywood is Barry Diller, chairman of the ailing 20th Century-Fox. Diller received $3 million a year for five years as basic pay.

He will, in addition, receive other compensation based on equity growth of Fox's parent company, TCF Holdings. Diller will receive 25 percent of any growth in cash. He will receive an additional cash payment of 17.5 percent of any equity growth in the three years which follow his five-year contract.

Only 14 executives in the entire United States receive a higher salary than Diller.

Diller's second in command, Lawrence Gordon, receives $750,000 salary, plus bonuses. Jonathan Dolgen, senior executive vice-president, and Harris Katleman, Fox's TV boss, receive $400,000 each.

Movie salaries are normally secret, but Diller's salary was revealed in a report to the SEC. The high salary was deemed necessary to woo him away from Paramount where he is rumored to have received $1 million a year, plus another $1 million in bonuses.

HIGHEST PAY PER SITCOM EPISODE

The highest salary per episode ever paid an actor in a Los Angeles-based situation comedy is believed to be the $225,000 per episode paid to Alan Alda for "M*A*S*H."

FIRST FOOTPRINT AT THE CHINESE THEATER

The very first footprint imprinted in the cement of the Chinese Theater (then Grauman's Chinese) in Hollywood was that of Norma Talmadge, who inadvertently stepped into a square of fresh cement that had not been roped off, and left her footprint. Sid Grauman, owner of the theater, took one look and a tradition was born.

ONLY ALIEN FOOTPRINTS AT CHINESE THEATER

Of the 170 footprints immortalized in cement at Grauman's Chinese Theater only three sets are of aliens: those of *Star Wars'* R2D2, C3PO, and Darth Vader.

SMALLEST FOOTPRINT

The smallest footprint at the Chinese Theater is that imprinted by Jeanette MacDonald, December 4, 1934. It measures six and a half inches from the tip of the toe to the outside of the heel. Roy Rogers's horse Trigger's hoofprint (April 21, 1949), which is nearby, measures five inches.

Visitors have long marveled at how tiny many of the stars' feet appear to be. It is now believed that in order to make their feet seem smaller, female stars, when the cameras weren't looking, took off their shoes and imprinted first the toe and then the heel closer than nature had provided. Did Jeanette do that? Only her podiatrist knows for sure.

LARGEST OPEN-AIR THEATER

The largest outdoor amphitheater is the Hollywood Bowl, which embraces 125 acres graced by hundreds of trees and shrubs and seats 17,619 music lovers.

EARLIEST CITY CHRISTMAS DECORATIONS

No city in California, and we hope, the world, ever decorated its streets for Christmas as early as did Hollywood in 1986 at the behest of Warner Brothers. Warner Brothers wanted to film Hollywood Boulevard with Christmas decorations, and they couldn't wait till Christmas. The Chamber of Commerce, which always cooperates with the film industry, agreed. Visitors to Hollywood Boulevard on a hot 83-degree day were stunned to see that famous promenade fully decked out with the bells and lights of Christmas on October 6, more than three weeks before Halloween. The film the early Christmas celebrated—*Lethal Weapon*.

HIGHEST PRICE PAID BY TV FOR A MOVIE

The highest price ever paid by a network for the television rights to a movie was $15 million, paid by CBS for the rights to *Star Wars*.

MOST STARS ON HOLLYWOOD BOULEVARD

The processes by which stars are chosen to be placed in the sidewalk for Hollywood Boulevard's Walk of Fame are mysterious. The Walk started in 1960 with eight stars and is administered by the Hollywood Chamber of Commerce. Names are added at the rate of about one a month. Celebrities must pay for the cost of engraving and installing their own stars. Current cost is $3,500.

No one in the Chamber of Commerce, which chooses the stars, can say why, but although there are 1,790 stars in Hollywood's Walk of Fame, three Academy Award winners—Jane Fonda, Dustin Hoffman, and Robert Redford—are not represented. Nor are Paul Newman and the Beatles. But Gene Autry and Tony Martin each have four stars.

LARGEST COSTUME SUPPLIER

The largest supplier of costumes for the movie industry is Western Costume Company of Hollywood. It was started in the old cowboy and Indian movie days by an Indian trader named L.L. Burns, who came to Los Angeles about 1912 and put his knowledge of Indian dress and customs to work designing Indian costumes for the western movies of cowboy William S. Hart. Western Costume has in stock more than one million costumes worth more than $25 million.

LARGEST FILM COMPANY

The largest film company in Hollywood is Paramount Pictures.

MOST MOVIES RELEASED IN A YEAR

The most full-length features ever released in a single year in Hollywood is 854, a record achieved by the movie industry in 1921 and never surpassed.

LARGEST MONSTER

The largest, most elaborate and expensive monster ever created is King Kong, a terrifying re-creation of the original movie monster made by Universal Studios especially for their tour. This Kong would have scared the pants off the original: he towers three stories into the sky and weighs seven tons. Even more scary, he cost $6.5 million, far more than the whole original picture. His home is Hollywood's largest sound stage, 100 by 160 feet and five stories high. Kong rises out of the East River, rips down power lines, attacks a full-sized helicopter, and attacks the tourists' tram as it crosses an almost full-sized Brooklyn Bridge. As a final horror, Kong blows on the passengers a hideous banana breath.

LARGEST PRODUCER'S OFFICE

More than 40 feet long, complete with fully equipped bar, 12 pipes on the desk, and an omnipresent butler, the office of mega-producer Aaron Spelling is quite properly the largest in Los Angeles. The Los Angeles *Times* states that a family of four could live comfortably in it.

STRANGEST MOVIE TYCOON PERK

Perhaps the strangest executive perk, bizarre even by Hollywood standards, was that of Mack Sennett of Keystone Kops fame. In order to be able to relax in hot water and thus get inspiration for his comedies, Sennett had a bathtub installed in the exact center of his office.

STRANGEST SUICIDE ATTEMPT

Before his marriage to movie sex symbol Jean Harlow, producer Paul Bern attempted suicide by flushing his head down the toilet. One of his rescuers was actor John Barrymore.

Bern is also reported to have tried, on his wedding night, to consummate his marriage with a dildo strapped to his waist. The marriage was a short one. Bern eventually succeeded at suicide with the unimaginative use of a gun.

FIRST MICKEY MOUSE

The first Mickey Mouse cartoon was conceived at the Disney Studios on Hyperion Avenue in 1928.

ONLY CITY NAMED AFTER AN APE MAN

Author Edgar Rice Burroughs, the creator of *Tarzan, the Ape Man*, lived in a section of Los Angeles that was eventually made into a separate political entity, and in honor of its most famous citizen's character, called itself Tarzana.

OLDEST THEATRICAL CLUB

The oldest theatrical club on the West Coast is the Masquers Club, founded in 1925 and located since 1927 at 1765 Sycamore. John Barrymore and W. C. Fields were among its early members.

MOST USED VOICE IN ANIMATION

The voice heard most frequently on Saturday morning and other times when cartoons are shown is that of Mel Blanc, who is the voice of Heathcliff, Bugs Bunny, Sylvester, Tweety Bird, Porky Pig, and Daffy Duck, among others.

MOST RELATIVES OF STARS WORKING ON A SINGLE TV SERIES

Hollywood has long been considered the world capital of nepotism, but no Hollywood project has ever had more relatives working on it than, believe it or not, "Believe It or Not." The television series employed 13 children or relatives of celebrities: Holly Palance, co-hostess with her father Jack Palance; Mark Davis, son of Sammy Davis, Jr.; Dennis Crosby, Jr., grandson of Bing Crosby; Mark Wolper, son of producer David Wolper; Jack Haley, Jr., son of the show's executive producer Jack Haley; Rory Flynn, daughter of Errol Flynn; Joe Luft, son of Judy Garland; William Schifrin, son of composer Lalo Schifrin; Barry Bregman, son of producer and musician Buddy Bregman; Peter Stuart, son of the show's producer Mel Stuart; Tom Fuchs, son of screenwriter Daniel Fuchs; Gloria Parnassus, sister of Jack Haley.

GHOST OF MOVIE STAR MOST OFTEN SIGHTED

For sheer box office value, no other Los Angeles area ghost comes close to that of the ghost of Lionel Barrymore, which still walks the many rooms of his mansion on Summit Drive, Beverly Hills, and is believed to have been seen many times. The present owner of the mansion, John Mercedes, a writer, claims he and his guests have seen Barrymore many times and report him to be amiable and nonthreatening. The ghost of Barrymore would probably have been considered more sensational by a generation not accustomed to reruns.

MOST DISTANT STAR

Genealogists have worked out that film star Humphrey Bogart was Princess Diana's distant cousin. They are seventh blood cousins.

MOST ELABORATE GRAVE OF A MOVIE STAR

The largest, most flamboyant grave of any movie star is

probably that at Hillside Cemetery in Baldwin Hills of singer-entertainer Al Jolson. The memorial includes an enormous statue of Al Jolson on his knees in his famous "Mammy" pose.

MOST EXPENSIVE MOVIE EVER PLANNED

The most expensive film ever planned was the L.A.-based Tri-Star production company's *Santa Claus*, budgeted at $50 million-plus. Other films may have hit that mark, but not intentionally.

ONLY ANIMALS ON WALK OF FAME

Only two dogs are on the Walk of Fame, Rin Tin Tin and Lassie.

COMPOSER OF MOST POPULAR WEDDING SONG

No woman composer has accompanied so many brides down the aisle as Los Angeles's Carrie Jacob Bons, the composer of "I Love You Truly."

She also wrote "A Perfect Day." Her home, which she named End of the Road, was built in 1917 and still stands at 2042 Pinehurst.

HIGHEST-PAID ANIMAL ACTOR

In her lifetime (actually there were several Lassies), the character Lassie earned more than any other animal in Hollywood history. Her last picture, *Magical Lassie*, paid her $100,000. The "Lassie" TV series was on for 20 years, ending in 1972. Toward the end of the series, Lassie was paid $3,750 per episode, plus $1,972 in reruns, plus a

$50,000 royalty, and from 10 to 40 percent of the profit for the vast merchandising revenues.

FIRST THEATER TO SHOW PLAYS

The first theater to show plays in the Los Angeles area was the Merced Theater at 418 N. Main Street. The theater was on the second floor and boasted only a 12-by-5-foot stage. The owners, William Abbott and his wife Merced, lived on the first floor. If the play died, they were prepared: the basement housed a mortuary.

The Merced became a saloon, a Methodist church, and an armory. It is currently undergoing yet another renovation, enjoying new status as a historical monument.

FIRST SWIMMING POOL

The first swimming pool in the Los Angeles area was built at Pickfair, the famous home of Mary Pickford and Douglas Fairbanks. It is located on the highest point in Beverly Hills and was big enough for Mary and Doug to go canoeing.

FIRST TECHNICOLOR FEATURE

The first technicolor feature film ever made in Los Angeles or, in fact, the world, was *Becky Sharp*, directed by Rueben Mamoulian in 1935.

FIRST SHOW-BIZ MOGUL TO GET A RAPE LAW CHANGED

In the early 1930s Alexander Pantages, the theater magnate, was accused of raping a woman, Eunice Pringle, who had come to his office applying for a job. His lawyers attempted to question the woman's chastity and moral reputation, but such questions were not permitted at that time under California law, and Pantages was convicted of rape.

However, Pantages's attorney, famed Jerry Geisler, appealed the verdict and got the law changed. Pantages was then acquitted.

BIGGEST HOLLYWOOD GOSSIP COLUMN LIE

In a profession noted for its inaccuracies, the top honor for a misstatement by a gossip columnist is credited to Dorothy Kilgallen. She once wrote a story claiming that Humphrey Bogart was having a relapse from a reported illness and was living on the eighth floor of the Los Angeles Memorial Hospital. It was a good thing for Bogey that he wasn't having a relapse, because, as he pointed out, not only isn't there an eighth floor in the Los Angeles Memorial Hospital, there is no Los Angeles Memorial Hospital.

MOST EXPENSIVE STAR'S BEACH HOUSE

The most expensive beach home ever sold in the Los Angeles area was to Johnny Carson for $9.5 million in 1983. The house, at Point Dume, Malibu, is ultramodern wood and glass and sits on two acres of beach front. It contains 11,000 square feet. It has four bedrooms and five bathrooms, sporting 24-carat gold fixtures. Space-age technology in the master bedroom controls the Levelors, the stereo, the security system, all indoor and outdoor lighting, and the closed-circuit TV. To relax in a day that's "so hot that..." Johnny has a swimming pool, a waterfall, a Jacuzzi, a koi pond, and a greenhouse.

HIGHEST COST OF A COMMERCIAL

Of all the television programs originating in the Los Angeles area, the highest price charged by a network for a commercial was the million dollars a minute charged for a commercial on a Super Bowl broadcast from the Rose Bowl.

BIGGEST LOSS ON A MOVIE

The biggest loss ever sustained on a movie is believed to be that suffered by United Artists in its production of *Heaven's Gate*, which Michael Cimino directed. Originally a medium-budget film, it took years to make and came in at a final figure of $57 million, including distribution and studio overhead. It lost $55.5 million.

Cimino, Hollywood's hottest "new" director, fresh from his triumph on *The Deer Hunter*, which won the Academy Award, was given extraordinary latitude, according to his producer Stephan Bach in his best-selling book *Final Cut*. Nobody wanted to see the four-hour-long picture. It was cut to three hours and thirty-nine minutes and still nobody wanted to see it.

FIRST MOVIE HOUSE ACOUSTICALLY ENGINEERED FOR SOUND

The first movie house in Los Angeles, indeed in the United States, to be acoustically engineered for sound was the Art Deco Cinema in The Casino in Avalon on Santa Catalina Island in 1930. The 1,200-seat theater, considered now to be the finest Art Deco movie house left in the United States, owed its prominence in history to three movie magnates: Cecil B. DeMille, Louis B. Mayer, and Sam Goldwyn, who used to sail their yachts to Catalina to preview their films.

MOST EXPENSIVE NONPEARLY GATES

The most expensive gates ever to adorn a local mansion were installed by singer Jermaine Jackson in his 1.9-acre estate (once owned by Johnny Weismuller) in Brentwood, for a quarter of a million dollars. The gates, personalized with an initialed crest, are replicas of those on the great estates in the St. Petersburg of the Czars.

The 16-foot-high gates were declared an eyesore by neighbors who demanded their removal, and Jackson was ordered to cut them in half to conform with local zoning. Conductor Zubin Mehta and his wife Nancy, who are neighbors, supported Jackson in the controversy.

LAST OF THE BIG FILM MOGULS

The last studio head to exercise total control over his product, to use only his own people with no outside help, to make deals with no independent producers, to reign as a supreme being in the manufacture of motion pictures until his death at age 65 (of cancer), was Walt Disney.

MOST PAMPERED SHOW-BIZ LAUNDRY

The world's most pampered laundry is probably that of Mark Goodson, the game-show packager, who, disdaining the several pages of laundries in the Los Angeles Yellow Pages, bundles his shirts, socks, and unmentionables from his Beverly Hills Hotel bungalow to a tried-and-true laundry close to his apartment in Manhattan near the United Nations.

LARGEST ADVERTISING SIGN

The largest advertising sign in the Los Angeles area and perhaps in the world is the HOLLYWOOD sign on Mt. Lee in the hills above Hollywood. The letters are 50 feet high.

Originally built in 1922 at a cost of $21,000, it advertised a subdivision called Hollywoodland. The "land" part of the sign slid down the hill leaving the rest of the sign to become one of the world's famous landmarks.

MOST FAMOUS CAR CRASH

The most written-about, talked-about car crash in Hollywood history was that in which actor James Dean lost his life. The circumstances so uncannily paralleled those of the movie in which he had just starred, *Rebel Without a Cause*, that his death created its own legends.

One of television's superstars, Ernie Kovacs, also was the victim of a deadly Los Angeles car crash, as was Jayne Mansfield, whose bizarre end came when the car in which she was driving with her boyfriend-lawyer tailgated a truck and she was decapitated.

LARGEST THEATER

When it was built in 1926 by the Ancient Arabic Order of Nobles of the Mystic Shrine as a modern version of 14th- and 15th-century Islamic architecture, the Shrine Auditorium was not only the largest theater in Los Angeles, it was the largest theater in the world. Originally having 6,489 seats, it has been renovated over the past few years and now holds 6,308 seats.

BIGGEST SUPPLIER OF LOOK-ALIKES

A Northridge company, Moe Thomas' Celebrity Look & Sound Alikes is the Los Angeles area's chief supplier of fake celebrities. The company lists 998 people who make their livings passing as celebrities. You can order a Marilyn Monroe, a Groucho Marx, a Charlie Chaplin, a Sylvester Stallone, or a John Travolta for your commercial or party.

FIRST MOVIE MADE IN HOLLYWOOD

The first movie shot in Hollywood was *The Squaw Man*, made in 1913 by Cecil B. DeMille, Samuel Goldwyn, and Jesse Lasky. It was filmed in a rented barn (Hollywood was largely agricultural in those days) at the corner of Vine Street and Selma Avenue.

Normally the picture would have been made in New York, but the producers headed west to avoid having to pay a royalty to Thomas Edison, who owned the patent on the movie equipment. Originally they had planned to shoot in Flagstaff, Arizona, but it was raining when DeMille arrived, so he decided to continue on to the end of the railroad line, which happened to be Hollywood, California. These movie pioneers liked not only Hollywood's climate, but the fact that it was close to the Mexican border if the law got too hot.

Like so much of Los Angeles crime, it paid well. *The Squaw Man* cost $15,000 and earned more than $250,000.

RICHEST PRIME-TIME PRODUCER

In the entire world no human being has produced more hours of prime-time television nor reaped greater financial rewards for doing it than Aaron Spelling, 63, of Beverly Hills. Spelling parlayed his first hit, "The Mod Squad" in 1968, to a packaging empire which has probably provided entertainment for more millions of people than any other private enterprise in history. His current wealth is judged to be about $235 million, but every time you see a rerun of "Charlie's Angels," "Love Boat," "Fantasy Island," or any other of his myriad shows, that figure ticks upward like the numbers on McDonald's golden arches.

MOST VISITED CEMETERY

The most visited cemetery in Los Angeles, and one of the most visited in the world, is Hollywood Memorial Park, immediately behind Paramount, where some of the most famous names in Hollywood are interred.

ONLY "WRITERS ONLY" COMPUTER STORE

Everybody in Hollywood has a movie they're writing, and now they're writing it on word processors. The Writers' Computer Store in west Los Angeles is the world's first establishment that will sell computers only to writers (others need not apply), and it has become so successful that a branch had to be opened in Studio City. Their secret: endless support for writers who are notoriously terrible with anything more mechanical than a pencil and call dozens of times a day with questions an accountant wouldn't dream of asking.

ALL-TIME TOP TV RATING

The highest rating ever obtained by a single L.A. television program was achieved in 1983 when the Los Angeles-based "M*A*S*H" attracted 77 percent of all the television sets in use for its final program.

The "Who Shot J.R.?" episode of "Dallas" in 1980 was a close second with a 76 percent share of the viewing audience.

"Roots" in 1977 scored at 70 percent.

All originated from Los Angeles.

OWNED MOST MOVIE STUDIOS

No man in Hollywood history is believed to have owned large parts of as many major movie studios as Kirk Kerkorian. He has owned, at one time or another, big chunks of MGM, Columbia, United Artists, and MGM/UA. What he owns currently depends upon when this book is read, but among other baubles in 1985 is 80 percent of the MGM Grand hotels. His present worth is somewhere above $600 million.

RICHEST PERSON IN SHOW BIZ

In choosing the richest person in show business, we have chosen to eliminate those whose fortunes were made largely in other pursuits and who appended the purchase of a studio or two to their list of holdings. The richest person must have devoted his life to the entertainment business and built his primary fortune in it. Many immensely wealthy film actors and actresses fill this requirement, and their names are among the best known in the world. Strangely enough, Hollywood's richest man in show biz does not come from this glittering peerage. His branch of show biz is at the bottom of Hollywood's pecking order, game shows. He gave the world "What's My Line?," "The Price Is Right," "Block Busters," "I've Got a Secret," "Family Feud," "Password," and "To Tell the Truth," among others. He is Mark Goodson of Beverly Hills and New York, whose net worth exceeds $300 million. He is the owner of more daily newspapers nation-wide than any other person in the Los Angeles area, perhaps in the country. But he leaves the operation to others and devotes himself to the daily, hands-on running of all his shows. He is known for his loyalty to his staff, some of them having been with him more than 30 years, fathers and sons sometimes working on the same shows.

RICHEST TALK SHOW HOST

No, it isn't Johnny Carson; it's Mervyn Edward Griffin with almost 23 years of continuously hosting the "Merv Griffin Show," cancelled in 1986. Merv's production company owns such historic hits as "Jeopardy" and "Wheel of Fortune," all of which he sold to Coca-Cola in 1986 for $200 million. Net worth: $235 million.

ONLY NETWORK TO EMPLOY A PSYCHIC TO PICK SHOWS

The only network to employ a psychic to help its president pick programs is ABC. From 1978 to 1980, ABC president Fred Pierce personally and secretly put psychic Beverlee Dean on the ABC payroll with a contract calling for $24,000 the first year, $30,000 the second to give him her psychic reactions to programs he was considering. When the deal was revealed, there was embarrassment all around and Dean was terminated. But in those two years ABC was number one in the nation and has not done as well since. "Mork and Mindy," "Benson," and "Taxi" were among the shows Beverlee picked to be hits.

RICHEST EX-AGENT

No man who started as an agent has accumulated more money and perhaps more genuine prestige than Lewis Wasserman, 73, of Beverly Hills, who once represented a stable of Hollywood's top stars, including Ronald Reagan. Wasserman made Universal one of the greatest studios on earth and himself a tidy bundle modestly estimated at more than $220 million.

RICHEST DISC JOCKEY

No disc jockey in history has ever enjoyed a financial success to equal that of Richard Wagstaff Clark, whose "American Bandstand," premiered in 1957, became one of TV's longest-running hits and whose Dick Clark Productions continues to produce such solid TV hits as "TV Bloopers." Clark, a combination of creativity, charm, and show-biz savvy, who at 56 looks 36, reigns over his kingdom with a benevolent nonchalance while sitting on a nest egg of some $180 million. In 1986 his company paid him a salary of $2.5 million.

Clark is the first man to host programs on three networks simultaneously: "25,000 Pyramid" (CBS); "American Bandstand" (ABC); and a radio show on NBC.

MOST EXPENSIVE SHOW-BIZ ACT

The most expensive show-business act in the world is the Rocket Man, who commands $10,000 for a 17-second flight which would come to $2,117,647 per hour.

The Rocket Man electrified the world when he blasted into the sky to open the Los Angeles 1984 Olympics. He flies wingless, with the rocket belt strapped to his waist and two tanks on his back filled with 90 percent pure hydrogen peroxide. He controls his flight with two motorcycle-type handle controls: speed with the right, direction with the left.

Only one rocket belt exists in the world but about 12 people have been trained to fly it. The pilot wears a burn-proof suit. He can make 60 miles an hour and usually jumps about 60 feet in the air.

MOST COSTLY NETWORK PROGRAMMING ERROR

The most disastrous judgment ever made by programming

executives occurred when ABC was offered the "Cosby Show." It had been produced by two former ABC programming chiefs, Marcy Carsey and Tom Werner, who were under contractual obligation to offer their output to ABC first. ABC studied the pilot and turned the show down. It was then offered to NBC which bought it, and the "Cosby Show" went on to become TV's most successful-ever sitcom.

Because of the effect the program would have had on the rest of its schedule, turning down the "Cosby Show" cost ABC an estimated half a billion to a billion dollars in revenue.

STAR WHO LOVED MOST FOOTBALL PLAYERS

No actress has loved football and football players more than Paramount star Clara Bow, the It girl of the 1920s and one of the first sex symbols. Miss Bow claimed that in one performance she had slept with the entire University of Southern California football team. When the story broke, her studio raised her salary to $5,000 a week. (USC was founded by Methodists to ensure spiritual values in higher education.)

BIGGEST FINANCIAL LOSS IN NETWORK HISTORY

The worst financial loss ever sustained by a network was that of ABC, which in 1986 posted a deficit of approximately $70 million, achieving the dubious distinction of being the first network ever to show a loss.

HIGHEST FEE PAID FOR SITCOM SYNDICATION

The most money ever paid for the syndication rights to a sitcom was for the "Cosby Show." In 1986 those rights were sold for a fee that will eventually come to somewhere between half a billion and a billion dollars.

MOST COSTLY TOUPEE

The most money ever paid by a Hollywood studio for a star's toupee was expended by Warner Brothers on a hairpiece confected for Sean Connery for the James Bond picture *Never Say Die*. The cost: $52,000, more than the entire cost of many early motion pictures.

BIGGEST INTERNATIONAL TV AUDIENCE

The biggest worldwide television audience is believed to be that of the 1987 Rose Bowl Parade which, in addition to a U.S. audience of 100 million people, was seen by 250 million people in 28 countries throughout Latin America, Asia, and Europe.

HIGHEST-PAID SCREEN STAR

The most money any star ever received for less than two weeks' work was the 18.5 million superbucks paid to Marlon Brando in 1978 for his twelve days' toil on *Superman*.

LARGEST OUTLET FOR STAR'S SECONDHAND CLOTHING

The only store selling solely clothes worn by celebrities is A Star Is Worn on Melrose Avenue. Each garment on the racks has a tag with the name of the star to whom the garment belonged and the price. Currently on sale: britches worn by Marlon Brando in *Mutiny on the Bounty*, $1,000; John Travolta's suit (autographed) from *Saturday Night Fever*, which he wore for a *Time* magazine cover, $2,500; Cher's leather studded pants (autographed), $625.00; Priscilla Presley's blue jacket, $35.00; Jaclyn Smith's silk shirt, $35.00.

The store accepts clothing from stars on consignment; the star's share of the sale is contributed to charity. Unless signed, clothing is less expensive than originally.

MOST SUCCESSFUL EX-ACTOR

The most successful ex-actor is Ronald Reagan, who went on from starring in mostly B-pictures to become a two-time governor of California and a two-time president of the United States, both jobs at a considerable cut in salary.

MOST SECRET DOCUMENT

No document is more secret—and more dreaded in Hollywood by performers—than an annual report called *TV-Q*.

TV-Q is compiled in large volumes that contain the names of almost every actor and actress and public figure in America. It stands for TV quotient. TV quotient purports to be able to measure an actor's recognition quotient and his likability quotient: how well the public recognizes him and how much it likes him.

TV-Q is so secret that many show-biz people believe it doesn't exist and, indeed, not one actor in a thousand has ever seen a copy. Most executives profess equal ignorance.

TV-Q is a major factor in casting. If a performer's TV-Q indicates he is not well known to today's audience even though he has made dozens of pictures or appeared in many series, he will not get the part. Worse—if he is well known, but if his TV-Q indicates the public does not like him (often a result of being cast as a character the public does not like) he certainly won't get the part. Neither of these two factors of course bears on his acting ability, which is why performers' unions hate *TV-Q* and management won't discuss it. No one is ever told he is turned down because of an inadequate TV-Q.

HIGHEST Q-POP

The highest Q-Pop (the TV-Q which measures popularity)

of any entertainer in America is that of Alan Alda—another way of saying he is the best-liked performer in the nation.

HIGHEST Q-POP OF AN ACTOR IN A CURRENT SERIES

As might be expected since his show is #1, the actor with the highest Q-Pop is Bill Cosby.

ACTRESS WITH HIGHEST Q-POP

The highest Q-Pop enjoyed by any actress with a series on the air is that of Betty White.

HIGHEST Q-POP OF A MALE MUSICIAN

The male music figure with the highest Q-Pop in America is Lionel Richie.

FEMALE MUSICIAN WITH HIGHEST Q-POP

The female musician with the highest Q-Pop in the nation is Whitney Houston.

LONGEST-REIGNING TV STAR

No performer in television history has held the same time slot against all competition for as long as Johnny Carson, who has remained king of late-night television for a quarter of a century.

Millions of dollars have been spent in vain attempts to dethrone him, and many major talents and grandiose ideas have failed. Among them: Joey Bishop, 1967; Dick Cavitt, 1970–1972; "Wide World of Entertainment," 1973; Merv Griffin, 1969–1972; Alan Thicke, 1985; Joan Rivers, 1986.

FIRST COMMERCIAL IN A HOME VIDEO CASSETTE

The first motion picture studio to insert a commercial in a home video cassette was Paramount, which placed an ad for Diet Pepsi in the cassette for *Top Gun*. The cassette was released March 11, 1987, a date which will live in infamy.

LARGEST EMPLOYER OF DEAD PEOPLE

The largest and possibly only employer of dead people in the Los Angeles area was Heaven's Union, founded in 1982 by Gabe Gabor, a Los Angeles entrepreneur. Heaven's Union was a messenger service designed to carry messages from the living to their loved ones who had died.

The cost was $40.00 for 50 words and included "... a beautiful certificate, suitable for framing, containing your message as a cherished remembrance."

Heaven's Union, through hospitals and hospices, contacted patients whose death in a short while was certain and employed them to carry the messages with them when they arrived at heaven or wherever. The messengers received $10.00 a message and were entrusted with as many as a hundred each, the theory being that once read the message would be registered upon the subconscious that survived into the spirit world.

Patients were reported eager for the job: it enabled a person to create an instant estate of $1,000 and gave the dying a new sense of purpose.

Gabor claims it's an old idea: the Incas would periodically designate a man as messenger, ply him with messages to the dead and, after a ceremony in his honor, toss him in a volcano.

The People

LOS ANGELES's glories are its climate and diversity of people who have wandered here enchanted by its beneficence and made the world colorful with movies, television, fads, fashions, and fancies: geniuses and heroes, rogues and apostates, they defy convention until suddenly the rest of the world catches up and the unconventional becomes conventional. Then proper people look again wistfully to Los Angeles to see what the city will be up to next.

AREA WITH MOST SMART PEOPLE

The Mensa Society, a national organization whose sole qualification for admission is a high I.Q., claims more members (612) in the San Fernando Valley than in any other part of Los Angeles.

Mensa admits members only after severe review to establish that they are indeed smarter than almost anybody.

SMARTEST KID TO VISIT DISNEYLAND

The smartest kid ever to visit Disneyland is believed to be Adragon Eastwood DeMello, who entered Cabrillo College at age eight and at age nine has already completed one year with a grade point average of 4.00.

In between visits to Disneyland (three times) he hopes to earn a Ph.D. in theoretical physics from Stanford when he is 14 and a second doctorate in astrophysics when he's 16.

His favorite ride at Disneyland is Tom Sawyer's Raft.

ONLY NUDE BEACH

At only one L.A. beach can one view in their entirety those beautiful bodies so patiently manufactured on the jogging trails and at the spas of L.A. Although not legally sanctioned, the beach is proudly touted by the Visitors and Convention Bureau. The city fathers look the other way; the city mothers don't look at all. The beach, designated as "clothing optional" is located just north of Point Dume and is known as Pirate's Cove.

In 1986, denizens of Venice picketed for their own nude beach.

MOST WANTED ITEM IN BEVERLY HILLS

Shoppers spent $662 million in taxable retail purchases in Beverly Hills in 1982. By far the greatest amount of that money, $143 million, was spent for clothes. Second: cars, $72 million.

An incredible $46 million was spent dining out, which

means that at 15 percent, waiters earned $6.9 million in tips.

OPTION CHOSEN BY MOST UNMARRIED TEENAGERS

Although popular opinion believes otherwise, 97 percent of all unmarried adolescent mothers in Los Angeles choose to keep their children.

SCHOOLING OPTION PICKED BY MOST TEENAGE FATHERS

The teenage father who drops out of school has become a cliché, but of all Los Angeles boys who become fathers in their teens, 70 percent finish high school.

MOST COMMON REASON GIRLS DROP OUT OF HIGH SCHOOL

Teenage mothers do not fare as well as their mates. The most common reason for dropping out of high school is pregnancy. Eighty percent of all Los Angeles teenage mothers never graduate from high school.

MOST SENIOR CITIZENS

Of all the communities comprising Greater Los Angeles, the one with the highest percentage of older people is Beverly Hills. This population is divided as follows:

Over 62	15,000
70–74	2,000
75–79	1,243
80–84	625
Over 84	329

The city has only one person working full-time for senior citizens.

MOST CENTENARIANS

Although the odds are 100 million to one against it, the Jewish Homes for the Aging of Greater Los Angeles had two residents, Moshe Abovitch and Annie Tahl, each celebrating their 101st birthday on the same day, January 9, 1987.

MOST BUREAUCRATS

The world's largest concentration of bureaucrats outside Washington D.C. is said to be in the public buildings around the downtown Civic Center area where federal, state, and local officials have their offices. Due perhaps to the evasive nature of politicians, no one has been able to come up with an exact count.

MOST LUXURIOUS HOME

Although the final honor of having produced the most luxurious house is always up for grabs, so many subjective judgments being involved, the house built by Everett Lobban Cord in Beverly Hills is accorded that distinction by more architects and designers than any other.

Cord, who produced the famous Duesenberg and Cord automobiles, two American classics, was determined to create an equal classic when he built his home. Located next to actor William Powell's own spectacular home, Cord's colonial-style mansion had 87 rooms in the main house with 36,000 square feet of walking space. The interior featured

Chippendale furniture, mahogany walls, white marble floors, and blue satin drapes. A curving marble staircase led to the cocktail loggia. A billiard room, shooting gallery, taproom, and organ chamber were located on the upper story. Mrs. Cord's bathroom was fitted with 14-carat gold fixtures.

Above the garage that accommodated 18 automobiles were five apartments for the servants.

In addition to a 100-foot-long swimming pool, the "play area" contained a playroom, dining room, kitchen, projection room for private movie screenings, and a mahogany dressing room.

WORST YEAR FOR SINGLE WOMEN

1984 was the worst year for single women in L.A.'s history. There were only 69.9 eligible men for every 100 eligible women—a figure which, incidentally, includes gays.

Only four other cities in the United States offer the ladies better odds.

SHORTEST HOTEL OWNERSHIP

The shortest ownership of a major hotel in the Los Angeles area was that of the Beverly Wilshire by real estate tycoon Bill Zeckendorf, who owned the grand hotel for a grand total of ten days before selling it to Hernando Courtwright in 1961.

PARTY WITH MOST REGISTERED VOTERS

The Democratic Party, as of February 1984, led L.A. County with 1,799,825 registered voters.

The Republicans were a distant second with 1,000,680.

Other parties: America Independents, 29,000; Peace and Freedom, 12,125; Libertarian, 17,512.

MOST EXPENSIVE SHOPPING CENTER IN THE WORLD

In their endless pursuit of the newest and most exclusive, shoppers have created in Beverly Hills the most expensive shopping center in the world, the Rodeo Collection, a small (66,000 square feet) but glittering multilevel array of expensive boutiques and restaurants on Rodeo Drive.

The shopping center mortgage tells the story. It was the largest loan per square foot in U.S. history, financed by one of the country's most conservative institutions, the John Hancock Mutual Life Insurance Co., which lent the developers $30 million. This averages out to $450 a square foot, two-and-a-half to three times the value of an average shopping center.

BIGGEST FISH EATERS

The largest consumers of seafood in the United States are Los Angelenos, who eat some $1.5 billion worth annually.

Although almost every restaurant claims it serves only fish that practically jumped into the boat that day, only 31 percent of the fish sold in Los Angeles is fresh. The fish probably wasn't even caught near Los Angeles. Ninety percent of all fish sold in California is imported from other states or countries.

LARGEST CAUSE OF AUTO DEATHS

Almost as many motorists kill pedestrians in Los Angeles as kill each other. In 1985, of 252 traffic deaths, the most, 91, were caused by moving vehicles hitting each other. The second leading cause of death was vehicles hitting pedestrians, which lowered the pedestrian population in 1985 by 82.

MOST LANGUAGES SPOKEN IN PUBLIC SCHOOLS

In 1985 the number of different languages spoken by Los Angeles's increasingly polyglot population reached a record number. There were, in that year, children in the public schools speaking a hundred different languages.

MOST MONEY SPENT PER STUDENT ON PUBLIC SCHOOL

The most money spent on each student by schools in the metropolitan Los Angeles area is the $1,200 per year spent in Beverly Hills.

LEAST MONEY SPENT PER STUDENT

The least money spent per student by a public school system in the Los Angeles area is $600 annually allocated by Baldwin Hills.

HIGHEST-PAID BANK EXECUTIVE

The most lushly compensated bank executive in Los Angeles and indeed in the whole United States is Bram Goldsmith, chairman of the Board of City National Bank, who steered his bank clear of many of the financial booby traps that have almost destroyed other banks, and accordingly receives a base pay of $701,422, plus a bonus and stock options that bring him to well over $1,000,000 a year.

MOST FREQUENT MAYORAL CANDIDATE

The most persistent candidate ever to aspire to the office of Mayor of Los Angeles is Eileen Anderson, who was also the first woman ever to run for the office. She launched her first mayoral campaign in 1969 and has been a candidate for the office in every election since.

She has also run for senator, representative, governor, City Council member, tax assessor, and Board of Education member, losing every time.

MOST POPULAR NAME FOR A DOG

There are 194,000 of man's best friend licensed by the Department of Animal Regulations in Los Angeles. The most popular name among the registered dogs is Lady, with 1,400 dogs answering to that name. Call "Here, Lady! Here, Lady!" in L.A. and anything can happen.

Next most popular name is Brandy.

MOST POPULAR DOG

The most popular breed in Los Angeles is the poodle. In 1983, L.A.'s licensed poodle population was 16,732, which is more than that of any other city in the United States.

LARGEST DOG SHOW

The largest dog show in the United States, next to the Westminster Show in New York, is the annual Beverly Hills Kennel Club Dog Show, which averages 2,760 competing canines.

Best of Show has been won most often (8 times) by terriers. Next, with three wins: Pekingese. Dobermans and Morgan Elk Hounds have each won twice.

RETURNS MOST LOST DOGS

No shelter in the Los Angeles area, and perhaps in the United States, is as successful in returning lost dogs to their owners as the Los Angeles County Animal Care Center in Agoura. In the 12-month period ending June 30, 1986, the Agoura shelter was able to return to their original owners 32 percent of all the dogs they had taken in (vs. 12 percent for L.A. city centers). Cats did not fare as well: neither the L.A. shelters nor the Agoura facility were able to return more than 1 percent of lost cats to their original owners.

SHELTER KILLING FEWEST DOGS AND CATS

It is an unfortunate fact of life that pets brought to an animal center, if not claimed or adopted, may eventually be killed. Nationally, the Humane Society estimates that 68 percent of all the dogs and 62 percent of all the cats are killed. In a 12-month period ending July 30, 1986, in Los Angeles city shelters, of the 47,934 dogs taken in, 61 percent were killed, and of the 32,934 cats 77 percent were killed. The best record for saving animals in the Los Angeles area and very possibly in the nation is that of the Los Angeles County Animal Care Center in Agoura. Of the 2,385 dogs taken in, it killed only 24 percent, and of its 1,423 cats, it killed only 20 percent.

MOST EXPENSIVE CAT

The most expensive cat ever offered for sale in Los Angeles is a new breed developed by a Hollywood man. Paul Casey, a former writer for *Lassie* scripts, combined eight different breeds from four continents (Siamese, spotted silver, Manx, Abyssinian, cat of the Nile, brown tabby, Malaya tropical house cat, and a spotted silver longhair) to produce a spotted house cat that looks like a miniature jungle animal but lives on your lap and is called California Spangled. It comes in silver, bronze, black, charcoal, gold, red, blue, or brown—plus a "snow leopard" which is born white and develops markings as it gets older. The 8–12-pound cats were featured as His and Her presents in the 1986 Neiman-Marcus Christmas catalog for $1,400 per cat.

MOST POPULAR BED

Despite rumors, Los Angeles is very traditional in the bedroom. Although Los Angeles is the water bed capital of the world with sales in 1982 of 225,000 units, ordinary spring and mattress beds account for 95 of every 100 beds sold.

LARGEST COLLEGE FUND DRIVE

In 1986, the University of Southern California announced a fund-raising goal of $557 million over the next 4 years. It was at that time the largest fund-raising goal ever set by a university. It has since been surpassed by another California university, Stanford, which in 1987 announced a goal of $1 billion.

MOST EXPENSIVE PLANE CHARTER

The most you can pay to charter an airplane in the L.A. area is $12,000 per peak hour, which will give you the services of a 727 with a crew of three pilots and one engineer. If you charter the same plane in off-times, it can cost you as little as $7,500 an hour.

A Lear Jet 35, which will carry eight passengers, will cost $1,200 an hour with two pilots. A Lear 24, which will carry six passengers, is only $1,000 an hour.

Instead of charging by the hour, smaller planes rent for so much per mile. A twin-engine turbo prop, which will carry nine passengers, is $2.15 a mile and gives you the services of two pilots. A nine-passenger twin engine Navajo Chieftain is $1.90 per mile. A twin-engine, five-passenger Cessna is $1.50 per mile. A single-engine Cessna, which carries five passengers, is $1.00 per mile.

MOST NATIVE AMERICANS

With a population of 100,000 Indians, the Los Angeles area is home to more native Americans than any other urban area in the United States.

MOST EXPENSIVE CHICKEN COOP

Everett Cord, the auto magnate, not only loved cars, he was crazy about chickens and built the most expensive chicken coop in the world as part of his Beverly Hills mansion.

The coop had mahogany walls, red brick floors, satin curtains, and gold vessels for chicken feed and water.

MOST EXPENSIVE COMIC BOOK

The most money that ever changed hands for a back-issue comic book in the Los Angeles area was for issue number 27 of Detective Comics, which featured the first appearance of Batman. The comic sold for $5,000.

In another notable transaction, in 1981 the owners of the

American Comic Book Company traded a 1938 comic book for a 1939 Ford Motor car.

MOST EXPENSIVE CONDO

The most expensive condominiums ever offered for sale in Los Angeles were two 6,500-square-foot penthouses in Wilshire House, a luxury high rise in the Wilshire corridor at 10601 Wilshire Boulevard. These two penthouses attained worldwide fame when, at the height of the real estate boom, they were offered for $11 million each, with a free Rolls-Royce thrown in. They each contain five bedrooms and seven and a half baths.

After a long dry period in which only ten of the building's 66 units were sold, the price was reduced to $5.3 million. The west penthouse in the building has been sold to an American businessman for $5 million. The remaining penthouse at $5.3 million is not L.A.'s most expensive current condo, but its biggest bargain. Where else could you buy a condo at a $5.7-million reduction?

MOST EXPENSIVE MOTOR YACHT YOU CAN CHARTER

The largest, most expensive motor yacht currently available for charter in the L.A. area is the 98-foot *Sun Star*, which charters for $3,025 per day or $15,550 per week. The yacht can sleep ten passengers in five private staterooms or can accommodate as many as one hundred for a party.

MOST EXPENSIVE SAILBOAT CHARTER

The largest and most expensive sailing yacht currently for charter in the L.A. area is the 78-foot New Zealand–built

Lady Jenny. Lady Jenny will sleep six, or it can accommodate 25 passengers for day sailing. She rents for $2,250 per day or $9,250 a week, including a crew of three.

MOST COMMON WAY TO OWN A ROLLS

Not all things in Los Angeles are what they seem, and most of those people tooling around in those luxury cars don't own them.

The most popular way to own a Mercedes-Benz (so common they are called Beverly Hills Chevies) or a Rolls-Royce is not to own it at all. A full 70 percent of all Rolls-Royces and Mercedes in Los Angeles are leased.

LARGEST RELIGION

The predominant religion in the Los Angeles area, with 2.37 million members, is Catholicism. Others: Jews, 500,000; Baptists, 172,777; United Methodists, 84,835.

In addition the area boasts Hindus, Buddhists, Mormons, Christian Scientists, and Greek Orthodox.

LARGEST IRS CLAIM AGAINST A TAXPAYER

The largest claim ever filed by the IRS against an individual taxpayer was against C. Arnhalt Smith for $22.8 million for his 1969 income tax.

LARGEST LAW FIRM

The largest law firm in Los Angeles is Gibson Dunn & Crutcher, 333 S. Grand Street, with 100 partners, 141 associates, and 470 nonlegal employees.

Second is O'Melveny-Meyers, 400 S. Hope, with 67 partners, 160 associates, and 472 nonlegals.

LARGEST GUN COLLECTION

The largest gun collection in the West belongs to the Ellis Mercantile Company, which has over 8,000 firearms, most of which are rented to movies and television.

The Ellis Mercantile Company, 169 North La Brea Avenue, is an independent prop house that also rents such things as coffins, presumably for the victims of their rented guns.

LARGEST COUNTY FAIR

The Los Angeles County Fair, held each September in Pomona, is the largest event of its kind on the North American continent. Every year over a million people visit the 487 acres with more than 200 permanent structures. More than 1,500,000 square feet of floor space is available for exhibitors.

LARGEST COCA-COLA MEMORABILIA STORE

The Real Thing in North Hollywood is not only the largest store of its kind in the Los Angeles area, but claims to be the only store in the world devoted exclusively to Coca-Cola memorabilia.

HIGHEST DIVORCE YEAR

The divorce rate peaked in Los Angeles in 1983, when one couple got divorced for every couple who got married, making L.A.'s divorce rate three times the national average.

HIGHEST DRIVING COSTS

According to the Hertz Corporation, Los Angeles is the most expensive city in the United States in which to drive a car.

GAYEST CITY

L.A.'s newest city, West Hollywood, was created by a referendum of voters in November 1984, on a ticket of gay rights and rent control. Of five councilmen elected at that time, three, including the woman mayor, were avowedly gay. Well within her first term, Mayor Valerie Terrigno was found guilty on 12 counts of embezzling $9,000 in federal funds while heading a counseling center and sent to jail.

BIGGEST TOY FAD

The biggest toy fad to originate in Los Angeles was the Hula Hoop, which went on to be the biggest toy fad in history.

The Hula Hoop was invented in Australia by a gym teacher who used it to keep her pupils fit. A then unknown toy company, Wham O Manufacturing Company, saw its possibilities and introduced it in brilliant plastic colors and sold 20 million the first year for a rumored profit of $45 million.

Later on, Wham O was to give the world the Frisbee.

MOST BUSINESS LICENSES

In glittering, world-famous Beverly Hills, the business for which the most licenses are granted is gardening.

RICHEST BLACK COMMUNITY

The wealthiest black community in Los Angeles, and considered one of the most attractive, is View Park in Baldwin Hills with houses ranging in size from 2,500 to 5,000 square feet and selling from $150,000 to $500,000.

Little known to either the general black or white public, View Park is located between La Brea Avenue and Crenshaw Boulevard, and has 2,000 large and beautifully landscaped custom-built Spanish colonial, Tudor, and ranch-style homes with views all the way to the Pacific Ocean.

FIRST DOG-WASHING DOGRAMAT

The first public facility for washing your dog is the Dogramat in Santa Monica, which supplies everything you need to wash your dog and charges by the dog-pound. The fee is $8.00 for short-hair dogs of less than 80 pounds and $10.00 for heavier ones: $10 to $20 for long-hair woofs.

For this you're provided with an elevated stainless steel tub, a bench with a rubber mat so Fido can jump into the tub, a wooden nonskid bathing platform, and a push-button spray hose with temperature controls. Also a blow dryer, although the owners recommend the dog be allowed to follow his natural instinct and shake himself dry.

ONLY CITY TO CANCEL CHRISTMAS

The city of West Hollywood became the first city to turn Grinch and steal Christmas. The City Council, in 1985, officially canceled Christmas as a city holiday and voted to keep the city hall open. To prove they meant it, the city gave out as Christmas presents to stunned citizens 200 parking tickets. A year later they bowed to public opinion and repealed the law.

LARGEST CONSUMER SHOW

The largest consumer show in Los Angeles, indeed the largest consumer show west of the Mississippi, is the annual Automobile Show, held every January at the Convention Center. The show racked up its greatest attendance in 1986 with 420,000 admissions in nine days. Six hundred cars were displayed.

MOST EXPENSIVE WOMEN'S PERFUME

The highest-priced perfume for women available in Los Angeles is the nationally distributed Joy, a floral Mimosa scent which sells for $445 per ounce.

LARGEST EMPLOYER IN LOS ANGELES

According to their figures, the Los Angeles–based company employing the most people worldwide is the Herbalife Company, which claims 800,000 salespeople.

MOST PUBLICIZED GARBAGE

Garbage tossed heedlessly into a trash bin in 1983 by a Mr. Peter Rooney has found its way to the United States Supreme Court and is allegedly the only garbage ever to reach that court. Rooney was alleged to be running an illegal bookmaking operation from his apartment on North Folores Street. Police, acting on a tip, searched the trash bin and found wager sheets with Rooney's name on them. On that evidence they arrested him.

Peter Rooney's attorneys contend that his garbage was protected from search by the Fourth Amendment. The prosecution countered that the Fourth Amendment was "intended for something more noble than the protection of discarded garbage." But the defense claims "a citizen abandons his garbage solely and only to his garbage man. A citizen should be protected from the policeman who rummages through the intimacies of personal life, be it discarded love letters, used contraceptives, discarded clothing, or similar articles."

In *California vs. Rooney*, 85-1835, the Supreme Court of the United States will decide once and for all: Is a man's garbage as sacred as his castle; can it be invaded without a warrant?

CHAMPION COUPON REDEEMER

So far as is known, no one has on a single supermarket shopping spree redeemed more coupons and received more free food than Joy Mosse, who lives in, of all places, Beverly Hills.

Ms. Mosse walked into a Safeway store at 4 P.M. one memorable October afternoon in 1986 and, working from a plan three pages long, bought paper products, canned goods, fresh produce, hamburgers, a beef roast, chicken breasts, and a pair of steaks for a total tape of $533.25. But Joy Mosse got it all free. All she paid was $24.12 in sales tax and enough coupons to require two hours at the checkout counter.

HIGHEST AUTO INSURANCE PREMIUMS

Someone once said "life is unfair," and nowhere is life more unfair than in the distribution of auto insurance premiums which in the Los Angeles area vary drunkenly from ZIP code to ZIP code and company to company.

Imagine a driver age 35–55, married, with no young children and no citations or accidents, driving a 1981 Buick Century worth $6,501 to $8,000 new. He wants an insurance policy with the following benefits: $100 to $250 deductible; liability $15,000/$30,000; $1,000 medical; and $15,000/$30,000 uninsured motorists. If he lived in Los Angeles ZIP code 90011 and bought his policy from SAFECO, he would pay the city's highest premium, $1,393 annually.

LEAST EXPENSIVE CAR INSURANCE

If the motorist who lived in ZIP code 90011 in Los Angeles and paid SAFECO $1,393 a year for auto insurance, the area's highest premium, were to move to Glendora and switch to Mercury Ins. Co., he would pay for the exact same coverage the L.A. area's lowest insurance rate, $390 a year.

CITY EMPLOYEES WITH HIGHEST ABSENTEEISM RATE

One hears of a bus driver's holiday and so far as is known, no other group of city employees seems to enjoy a day off quite so much as L.A.'s bus drivers, who in 1986 chalked up the highest rate of absenteeism ever enjoyed by any group of city employees. Every day, 13 percent of RTD drivers were away on unscheduled absences.

Besides a paid vacation and paid holidays, the average RTD driver treated himself to another 32 days of leave.

And one out of five bus drivers stayed out 80 extra unauthorized days, which is believed to be a city and probably a world record for absenteeism.

MOST DANGEROUS BUSES

According to the figures reported by the bus company to the federal Urban Mass Transportation Administration, Los Angeles's RTD has the worst accident record among the nation's ten largest transit agencies, 7.41 accidents per 100,000 miles.

MOST PEOPLE PER SQUARE MILE

The greatest population density in Los Angeles is that of the Rampart district, which encompasses an area of 11.7 square miles and has a population of 21,430 people per square mile.

FEWEST PEOPLE PER SQUARE MILE

Despite the proliferation of high rises, the lowest population density to be found in Los Angeles is in the wide open spaces of West L.A., whose 64 square miles is home to a mere 3,084 persons per square mile.

MOST PEOPLE KILLED BY A CHEESE

The most people ever killed in a food-caused epidemic in the United States died in 1986 of listeriosis caused from eating a cheese used mainly in Hispanic cooking. The killer cheese claimed 40 lives.

LARGEST LANDOWNER IN L.A. COUNTY

The largest landowner in Los Angeles County is the federal government, with 763,237.20 acres. Federal, state, and county governments among them own 39.15 percent of the land.

LARGEST DEFENSE CONTRACTOR

The largest defense contractor in Los Angeles in 1982 was Rockwell Corporation with $2 billion in defense contracts, basically for fixed-wing aircraft.

LOWEST-PAID MAYOR

The mayor of Beverly Hills is believed to be the lowest-paid mayor of any city of similar size and fame. His salary, which would barely buy him a suit on Rodeo Drive, is $3,128 a year.

LARGEST CORPORATION

The largest corporation headquartered in Los Angeles (and the 12th largest in the U.S.) with revenues in 1984 of $24,654 million is the petroleum giant, Atlantic Richfield.

LONGEST-RUNNING BLOCK PARTY

Once a year the neighbors get together and party in the street at what they call the Linda/Orum block party in Bel Air. The event has been held annually for the past 34 years and is believed to be the longest-running such festival in Los Angeles.

STINGIEST CITIZENS

In terms of giving, Los Angeles has the worst United Way record in the area and ranks next to last among the 12 largest United Way regions. The current per capita gift in Los Angeles is $10.03.

FIRST POST OFFICE WITH VALET PARKING

The first post office in California and perhaps in the world to offer to park your car for you is the Beverly Hills Post Office, which, in September 1986, inaugurated valet parking.

An attendant with white shirt and tie will take your car and park and retrieve it for you for 50 cents for 20 minutes with validation to prove you at least bought a stamp.

CHEAPEST OVERNIGHT ACCOMMODATIONS

The cheapest place to stay in Los Angeles is at one of its three Youth Hostels located in Hollywood (35 beds), Westchester (50 beds), and Harbor City (60 beds). Hollywood is $8.00 per night; Harbor City $6.25. Despite their titles, the Youth Hostels welcome visitors of all ages.

MOST MONEY EVER COLLECTED WITH A TIN CAN

A little old lady, 4 feet 11 inches and 91 pounds, now wearing a pacemaker and suffering from diabetes, has been standing outside Canter's Deli on Fairfax Avenue daily for the past 23 years, shaking a tin can and asking for money for the Jewish National Fund. According to that charity, Sylvia Orzoff, 77, has collected, mostly in single dollar bills and coins, an astounding $2.5 million.

BIGGEST NATURALIZATION CEREMONY

The most new citizens ever naturalized in a single ceremony in Los Angeles were sworn in at the Memorial Coliseum in 1981 when 10,000 people, representing some 94 countries, took the oath of citizenship.

MOST NATURALIZATIONS IN A SINGLE WEEK

The record for the number of aliens ever naturalized in a single week in Los Angeles was set in November 1985, when 70,000 new citizens took the oath of allegiance to their new country.

MOST RUSSIANS NATURALIZED

The most immigrants from the Soviet Union ever inducted in a single ceremony were 175 Russians who took the oath of citizenship in September 1986.

MOST MOBILE HOMES

Although Los Angeles appears ringed with mobile home parks, popular perception is that none exists within the city itself. The opposite is true. L.A. has more mobile homes than any city in the area, with 6,500 spaces in 68 parks scattered from the San Fernando Valley to San Pedro to the Pacific Palisades.

Mobile homes are particularly handy in Los Angeles: they give you a place to live while you're looking for a place to park.

SEVEN BEST DOCTORS IN LOS ANGELES

The word *best* is not normally used in this book because the term implies a value judgment, not a fact. However, we feel permitted to quote the facts of a study made in 1984 by *Good Housekeeping* magazine to determine the best doctors in the United States. *Good Housekeeping* asked 400 department chairmen and clinical chiefs at 87 medical schools which doctors they considered the best in their fields. Of all the doctors in the United States, seven in Los Angeles made the list, and we present them, but with the qualification that the list is not ours.

BEST GYNECOLOGIST-OBSTETRICIANS

Howard L. Judd, M.D., Chief, Division of Reproductive Endocrinology, UCLA Medical School

Leo D. Lagasso, M.D., Chief, Gynecological Oncology, UCLA Medical School

BEST ORTHOPEDIC SURGEON

Harlan Amstutz, M.D., Chief of Orthopedics, UCLA Medical School

BEST UROLOGIST

Joseph J. Kaufman, M.D., Chief of Urology, UCLA Medical School

BEST PLASTIC SURGEON

Jack Sheen, M.D., Department of Plastic Surgery and Reconstructive Surgery, UCLA Medical School

BEST OTOLARYNGLOGIST (EAR, NOSE, THROAT)

Howard P. House, M.D., Chairman, Emeritus, Founder, House Ear Institute USC Medical Center

Dr. William F. House, M.D., President, House Ear Institute, USC Medical Center.

ONLY L.A. SLAVE

Records show that only one slave was ever owned in the

Los Angeles area. History tells us nothing about him, save for a cryptic note that he was sold 52 times a year for as long as he lived.

No one today seems to know why.

ONLY DENTIST WITH CITY NAMED AFTER HIM

The only dentist in the Los Angeles area, and perhaps in the world, to have a city named after him is David Burbank, D.D.S., one of the codevelopers of Burbank. It was the dentist who gave his name to the city and not horticulturist Luther Burbank as some people think.

ONLY CANE STORE

The Boserup House of Canes at 1636 Westwood Boulevard in West L.A. claims to be the only store in the world specializing entirely in canes. It stocks 1,500 varieties ranging in price from $10 to $1,000.

OLDEST JEWISH CONGREGATION

The oldest Jewish congregation in Los Angeles is that of the Wilshire Boulevard Temple, which was constructed by the B'nai B'rith at 3663 Wilshire Boulevard and dedicated in 1929. It is one of the largest and most influential Reformed congregations in Los Angeles.

MOST SACRED SPOT TO INDIANS

The Shrine of the Self-Realization Fellowship on Sunset Boulevard near the Pacific Ocean is the most sacred spot in the Los Angeles area to people from India. A sarcophagus from China contains some of Mahatma Gandhi's ashes.

MOST UNCLAIMED TAX REFUND CHECKS

California leads the nation in the number of unclaimed tax refund checks with 12,755 checks, which are worth $6.6 million. Most of the money is due Los Angelenos.

MOST UNDOCUMENTED ALIENS

In the last ten years, Los Angeles has absorbed more undocumented aliens than any other American city has in the last 80 years.

MOST ILLEGAL ALIENS

Of the one to two million illegal aliens estimated to live in the Los Angeles area, the most, at least one million, are believed to be of Hispanic origin.

MOST SCHOOL DROPOUTS

The highest dropout rate in the Los Angeles school system, the nation's second largest, is that of the Latino segment, chiefly Mexican-Americans and Puerto Ricans. Forty percent leave before the tenth grade.

Of the Mexican-Americans and Puerto Ricans who do enter high school, 45 percent never finish. Of Anglo students, 17 percent fail to finish high school.

MOST HISTORIC SPOT

The most historic spot in Los Angeles is not the drugstore where Lana Turner was allegedly discovered, but an adobe home in the Hollywood Hills where the peace treaty which ended the Mexican–American War was signed in 1847.

Only the site now remains at 1903 Outpost Drive. It had

once been owned by General Harrison Otis, the founder of the Los Angeles *Times*.

LARGEST ANTIDRINKING ORGANIZATION

The Women's Christian Temperance Union of Southern California is the area's largest temperance organization and the largest WCTU chapter in the United States. It has approximately 1,500 members and directs its efforts toward educating young people against the use of alcohol and drugs.

FIRST WOMAN POLICE REPORTER

Back in 1914 when women were barely tolerated in newspaper offices as secretaries, William Randolph Hearst took the daring move of hiring Adela Rogers St. Johns to be the country's first woman police reporter on his Los Angeles *Herald*. She went on to become an internationally acclaimed writer.

FIRST PUBLIC SCHOOL

In 1854 with 500 school-age children living in the city and a surplus of $3,000 in the budget, the City of Los Angeles built the first public school. It was a two-story building at Second and Spring Streets.

FIRST McDONALD'S

The first McDonald's in the world was a hamburger stand opened by a pair of theater owners, Maurice and Richard McDonald, near Pasadena in 1940.

In 1948, they turned it into a self-service restaurant with

such success that a restaurant equipment entrepreneur, Ray Kroc, was enlisted to sell franchises. By 1960 there were 200 outlets. Kroc eventually bought out the McDonald brothers for $2.7 million.

FIRST MAP OF LOS ANGELES

The first map ever of Los Angeles was made for the Army in 1849 for a total cost of $3,000.

Broadway was called Fort Street because it led to Ft. Moore.

Spring Street was named by cartographer Lt. E. O. Ord for his girlfriend, whom he called "My Springtime."

The western boundary of Los Angeles was Figueroa, Spanish for Street of Grasshoppers.

FIRST HOME IN BEVERLY HILLS

When Barton Green, an oil explorer, couldn't find oil on some unnamed acreage in Los Angeles, he subdivided the area for homesites, built a house there for himself, and named the area Beverly Hills after his home town, Beverly Farm, Massachusetts.

FIRST IRS DOOR-TO-DOOR TAX SWEEP

On August 23, 1953, a special team from the IRS ran the first local door-to-door tax survey in Beverly Hills and audited every tax return in town. The sweep yielded $6 million in taxes on undeclared income or disallowed deductions. No one in Beverly Hills has slept well since.

FIRST BEVERLY HILLS DWELLERS

The original inhabitants of what is now Beverly Hills

were the Gabrielinas, a tribe of Indians who were less than five feet tall.

The Spanish bought the area from them for a handful of beads, making it an even better bargain than the Dutch got for Manhattan.

Once the Spanish took over under Father Junipero Serra, the Gabrielinas are said to have begun to kill themselves, the suicide toll ultimately reaching 1,000.

FIRST CEMETERY

The first cemetery in the Los Angeles area was located adjacent to the Plaza Church at 521 North Main Street. It was used from 1823 until 1844 to inter the remains of such diverse groups as the area's aboriginal inhabitants of Yang-Na, the Gabrielino Village, and early Spanish and Mexican settlers.

It is now a parking lot. For cars.

FIRST AUCTION OF UNWANTED TIME-SHARE VACATIONS

Buyers who were stuck with time-share vacations, which they couldn't use and couldn't sell, found an outlet to unload their grief at the first-ever auction of unwanted time-share vacations held at the Los Angeles Convention Center in February 1985.

The auction rules guaranteed that the sellers would have a loss and the buyers a bargain. The rules stated that the seller must offer the time-share for a maximum of 50 percent of its purchase price. A buyer, for instance, who paid $8,000 for a time-share plan had to agree to sell it for $4,000 if no higher bid came along.

Since time-shares are almost impossible to sell through

normal real estate channels, the time-share auction promises to become an annual or semiannual affair and to spread to other cities.

MOST PROFITABLE REAL ESTATE BUY

In 1850 Major Henry Hancock and B.D. Wilson purchased a four-thousand-acre ranch called Rancho de Las Aquas for $3,000.

That $3,000 ranch today is the city of Beverly Hills.

BIGGEST BANK FAILURE

The biggest bank failure in U.S. history was that of the U.S. National Bank of Los Angeles, which lost $398.4 million due to the Manipulations of C. Arnholt Smith, who is immortalized elsewhere in this book as one of history's greatest swindlers. Smith bought the ailing Fidelity Bank of Beverly Hills and made it a subsidiary of his Westgate-California conglomerate, which included an airline, tuna fleet, cannery, hotel, insurance company, produce wholesaler, and the San Diego Padres.

Smith's empire also included the U.S. National Bank of Los Angeles, the ninth richest bank in California and the 86th richest in the country.

It was declared insolvent on October 18, 1973, precipitating a gut-wrenching run at the bank with long lines of frantic depositors. No depositor lost money, but the bank's shareholders lost their investments.

Crocker National Bank took over the U.S. National branches.

FIRST SPANISH PHONE BOOK

The first all-Spanish phone book ever issued in the L.A.

area is the Spanish Yellow Pages, Las Paginas Amarillas de Pacific Bell.

The book lists 259,000 Hispanic homes and businesses which are part of what Pacific Bell calls the fastest-growing market in Los Angeles County.

LARGEST BLACK NEWSPAPER

The largest black newspaper in Los Angeles and the second largest in the United States is the L.A. *Sentinel*, a weekly that at one time had attained a circulation of 56,000 and now has an average of 25,000.

Once an advertising throwaway, the paper became famous in the 1930s with its slogan, "Don't spend where you can't work," a campaign to force white-owned businesses to hire blacks.

In 1986 a national association of 128 black-owned newspapers named the *Sentinel* the second-best black newspaper in the country.

BIGGEST HOME REMODELER

The largest home remodeler in the Los Angeles area is Pacific Builders, a 60-year-old firm specializing in room additions, kitchens, and second-story additions.

More home remodeling is done in Los Angeles than in any other city in the country. In 1985 the dollar amount was $611 million, almost three times that of the next highest city.

NUMBER-ONE INVESTMENT

In Los Angeles, indeed in the whole state of California, more money is invested in cars than in any other item, including houses, which are second.

MOST ROLLS-ROYCES

Los Angeles has more licensed Rolls-Royces than any other city in the United States—more than 3,000.

MOST ELABORATE WINE CELLAR

A certain mystery surrounds it, but the most elaborate wine cellar ever built in the Los Angeles area is believed to be a "designer wine cave" installed in a $6.5 million oceanfront house in Newport. The wine cave boasts a wine-tasting room and holds 5,000 bottles of wine.

Its architect is said to be the genius who designed Disneyland's Pirates of the Caribbean.

MOST EXPENSIVE STORE

The most expensive store in the world is Bijan on Rodeo Drive in Beverly Hills. Bijan's customer list is more closely guarded than our atomic secrets, and every clerk allegedly has orders to chew it and swallow it in case of invasion by reporters.

However, be you prince or producer or movie star, there'll be some little bauble to catch your fancy—say a basic little suit with gold pinstripes, knocked down at $11,500. Or for the man who has everything except a pleasing aroma, how about a bottle of perfume, enshrined in Bacarrat crystal and on sale at only $1,500?

For the truly chic, whose elegance may have created enemies, Bijan offers a chinchilla jacket for a lifesaving $27,000. It's bulletproof.

BIGGEST BANK PROFITS

The biggest profit shown by any bank on the West Coast,

indeed the biggest profit shown by any multinational bank in the United States, is that earned by Security Pacific, which over a five-year period averaged 16.1 percent earnings on shareholders' investments.

MOST EXPENSIVE GIFT ITEM IN A CHRISTMAS CATALOG

Not even Neiman-Marcus, noted for offering such conspicuous consumer goodies as His and Her helicopters in its Christmas catalog, has come even close to the opulence of the dream gift offered by Robinson's department store in its 1984 catalog.

The catalog offered an entire art museum, complete with a selection of 18th-century rococo paintings. "Give the gift of art, and savor the magic moment forever," says the catalog. "Possess art treasures of international renown and a personal museum worthy of their beauty."

The museum will be constructed on your lot (not included in the purchase price) and designed by famous architect Michael Graves. The museum encompasses about 5,000 square feet, the approximate size of a modest mansion, if there be such a thing. The cost: $19,749,000. That's about $2 million for the museum and just under $18 million for the paintings. The price doesn't include gift wrapping.

As of 1986, there had been no takers.

MOST EXPENSIVE STREET

Nowhere in the world has the man or woman with a princely pocketbook an opportunity to spend so much money in so few steps as on Rodeo Drive in Beverly Hills. This is the most expensive single block of shops in the world.

Gucci, Bijan, Tiffany, Giorgio, and other beloved bazaars of the international big bucks bunch stand glittering show window to show window in the earth's most concentrated invitation to conspicuous consumption: $100 T-shirts and $10,000 evening dresses, no more than a limousine length apart.

LARGEST LOSS OF TOP-SECRET DEFENSE DOCUMENTS

When a top-secret document is lost, everyone concerned tries to keep the loss itself top secret so it is impossible to say for certain which is the largest, most catastrophic loss that ever occurred. But certainly the largest admitted loss of top-secret documents in the Los Angeles area, and perhaps in all United States history, is that charged against Lockheed Corporation by a House of Representatives subcommittee.

Lockheed, the committee says, lost 1,400 documents dealing with a project which is described as so secret that the Defense Department will not even admit it exists. Some of the documents have been missing three years.

OLDEST NEWSBOY

The oldest newsboy regularly selling newspapers on a street corner in Los Angeles is Leslie Lewkowitz, 87, who has been a newsboy for 71 consecutive years, the last 43 on the same corner, La Cienega and Pico. He still puts in a full 12-hour day, 6 A.M. to 6 P.M., selling the L.A. *Times*, *Herald Examiner*, Santa Monica *Outlook*, *La Opinion*, *Noticias del Mundo*, and the *Daily Racing Form*.

LEADING PEDDLER OF JUNK BONDS

The chief architect of the $120-billion junk bond market

and the man who has sold more of them than any person is Beverly Hills's Michael Miliken, 40, senior vice-president of Drexel-Burnham Lambert Inc. Miliken is a fabled workaholic whose 18-hour days have brought him a fortune estimated in the hundreds of millions.

FIRST BLACK MAYOR

Although Tom Bradley is generally credited with being the first black mayor of Los Angeles, the first black mayor was, in fact, Juan Francisco Reyes, who from 1793 to 1795 served as Los Angeles's Alcalde (Spanish for mayor).

Reyes was officially listed in the census as mulatto, a mixture of Spanish and black. During his term the population of Los Angeles was 80 families.

MOST MEDIUMS

No city in the United States it is believed has as many mediums as Los Angeles. Ten years ago the city had two; today it has an estimated 1,000.

These mediums, or channels as they are called today, are men and women who never considered themselves to be other than ordinary but who suddenly are finding out they can put themselves into a semiconscious or unconscious state and communicate with someone they believe to be from the spirit world, not necessarily a dead person. It can be an extraterrestrial or even the collective unconscious of mankind. The spirit, speaking through the channel, will discuss life, predict the future, answer questions on health, love, business, or virtually anything. Limited studies show that most channels had traumatic childhoods. Channeling parties are currently enormously popular among many of the Los Angeles affluent.

FASTEST-GROWING ETHNIC GROUP

Although Hispanics will most likely be the largest ethnic community in Los Angeles by the turn of the century, the fastest-growing population is the Asian populace, which is expected to triple in the 30 years from 1970 to 2000.

LARGEST SCHOOL DISTRICT

The Los Angeles Unified School District, with 618 schools and 579,000 students, is the largest in California and second largest in the United States.

YOUNGEST MAYOR

The youngest mayor ever elected in the Los Angeles area is Gilbert Saldana, scion of the largest family in Avalon on Santa Catalina Island.

Saldana, whose mother runs the post office and his father the barber shop, started in politics at age 15. At 19, while still a student at California State University, Long Beach, he was appointed to the Avalon Planning Commission. At 23 he was mayor.

OLDEST SIAMESE TWINS

The oldest Siamese twins in the Los Angeles area are Yvonne and Yvette Jones, who are joined at the head. They were born in 1949 and were still living as of 1986.

They are said to have refused an operation which is relatively safe and could have separated them.

MOST ASIAN-OWNED BUSINESSES

Nowhere else in the United States do as many Asians,

American-Indians, and other nonblack, non-Latino minorities own their own businesses as in the Los Angeles–Long Beach area, where 38,331 individuals own their own businesses—almost double that of the next city, Honolulu.

MOST BLACK-OWNED BUSINESSES

More blacks own their own business in the Los Angeles–Long Beach area than anywhere else in the United States. They own 23,520 businesses, surpassing the next area, New York–New Jersey, by about 11 percent.

MOST LATINO-OWNED BUSINESSES

In no other city in the United States do as many Latinos own their own businesses as in the Los Angeles–Long Beach area, where they own 298,982 enterprises. They surpass the next city, Miami, by 20 percent.

LARGEST SOCIETY LUNCHEONS

The largest luncheons given regularly by a society matron in her own house were those confected by Mrs. Henry Winchester Robinson, whose father-in-law founded Robinson's Department Stores. Her mansion, built in 1911 above the Beverly Hills Hotel, was a society landmark, and even when she was in her late nineties, Mrs. Robinson continued giving weekly luncheons with seldom less than 90 guests.

LONGEST JOB LINE

In 1984, an advertisement in the Los Angeles *Times* for 350 longshoremen produced 20,000 applicants who showed up in cars and vans in a line that stretched for ten miles. Longshoremen with proper seniority, etc., can top out at almost $50,000 a year.

BIGGEST IMPORTER OF MEXICAN ARTIFACTS

Starting 19 years ago, at the age of 19, standing on the corner of Hollywood and Vine selling knickknacks he had brought back from Mexico in his car, Jerry Stofferz has built his business, Arte de Mexico, into the nation's largest importer of Mexican artifacts.

HIGHEST ALIMONY

The largest alimony claim ever filed in Los Angeles was by Beverly Hills resident Sheika Dena Al-Fassi, who asked $3 billion from her ex-husband, Sheik Mohammed Al-Fassi.

Since Sheika Dena was 23 and her husband, the sheik, 28, this was hardly part of community property they had accumulated since marriage.

The sheik is part of the Royal Family of Saudi Arabia. The court awarded his wife $81 million, with which she professed great satisfaction.

LARGEST MARCHING BAND

The largest marching band in Los Angeles history was organized by the L.A. Dodgers and played in Dodger Stadium on April 15, 1985, under the direction of Danny Kaye. The band was composed of 3,182 musicians and featured 1,342 majorettes, standard bearers, and drill team members. The total: 4,524 students from 52 high schools in the L.A. area.

MOST DRAFT EVADERS

During the 12-year involvement of the United States in Vietnam, Beverly Hills had more draft deferments per capita than any other city in the United States. Only 333 of 9,000 draftable-age men during that period went to Vietnam, leading some people to refer to the young men of that city as the Beverly Hills Dodgers.

Beverly Hills doctors are said to have certified draftable youths as drug addicts and homosexuals. There were also a mass of early weddings and swift pregnancies.

LARGEST EMPLOYMENT DISCRIMINATION AWARD

The largest sum of money ever awarded to a victim of discrimination in the Los Angeles area and perhaps the nation was the $1 million-plus settlement won by a black engineer as the result of a five-year lawsuit against the Department of County Engineer facilities. The court found he had been the victim of a long history of quiet prejudice that eventually led to his demotion and dismissal.

RICHEST MAN

The wealthiest man in the Los Angeles area, and its only billionaire, is Marvin Davis, 61, of Beverly Hills. The frequency with which the word *billion* appears in defense budgets should not cause us to lose respect for it. A billion is truly an awesome amount when it is the property of a single human being. A billion dollars is a thousand million ($1,000,000,000). At 10 percent—and a man clever enough to amass a billion will probably do much better—Mr. Davis would have an income of $100 million a year or about $2 million a week. If Mr. Davis spent $400,000 every day the stores are open, he could shop every day of his life and never touch his original billion dollars. In 1982 the income of the entire United States government was only $602 billion. Put 602 Marvin Davises together, and you would have had enough money to run the entire United States for all of 1982.

Marvin Davis comes from a pretty well heeled but nonmegabuck background: his father was in women's dresses—as the joke goes. Marvin made his first fortune in oil as the wildest of the wildcatters (known as Mr. Wildcatter), moved into real estate, and bought and sold with a knack for getting out just before things crashed.

He is best known in Los Angeles for his wildcatting in the movie industry, having once owned 20th Century-Fox. He is listed by Forbes as the 11th richest man in the country.

RICHEST HIGH SCHOOL DROPOUT

The richest high school dropout, and indeed the second richest man in the whole Los Angeles area, is David H. Murdock, 64, of Bel Air.

Mr. Murdock made his fortune by being a genius in the arcane worlds of high finance, oil, construction, buyouts, etc. His net worth: more than $650 million. Heaven knows what he would be worth if he had finished high school.

WEALTHIEST EX-ATHLETE

Although his disappointment at missing out on the 1956 Olympic team for which he was considered a prime candidate was crushing at the time, Newport Beach's Donald Leroy Bren with the true grit of millionaires went on to become the Los Angeles area's third richest man, with a real estate fortune (which includes some 68,000 acres of buildable land in Orange County) estimated at more than $600 million.

YOUNGEST HALF-BILLIONAIRE

Only five men in the L.A. area have made it to the half-billion-dollar mark. The youngest of these is Michael R. Milken of Encino who via a combination of cheerleader personality, inspiration, and perspiration applied to such things as junk bonds and real estate has made himself a half-billionaire at age 40.

WEALTHIEST PUBLISHER

No world-class magazine publisher came from such humble beginnings and amassed so great a fortune as one-time auto mechanic and short-order cook Robert E. Peterson, 61, of Beverly Hills.

Mr. Petersen started *Hot Rod* magazine on a few hundred bucks after World War II and built that magazine into an empire which embraces 13 monthlies aimed mostly at kids or blue-collar readers: *Motor Trend, Guns & Ammo*, etc. A guns and ammo man himself, he has hunted wild boar in Poland and polar bears in Alaska. His net worth is about $235 million.

MOST INHERITED WEALTH

Los Angeles is a young city and most of the megabuck fortunes were earned rather than inherited. The biggest concentration of inherited wealth belongs to three sisters who inherited the estate of Burton Green, the developer of Beverly Hills. The three Green girls, Dorothy Green, Liliore Green Raines, and Burton Green Bettingen, septuagenarians all, of Beverly Hills, have a combined wealth of somewhere near three-quarters of a billion dollars.

WEALTHIEST ART COLLECTOR

The wealthiest art collector in Los Angeles is a Berkeley dropout, industrialist Norton Simon, 79, chief benefactor of the museum in Pasadena which bears his name. His art and industrial holdings put him in the $200-million bracket.

RICHEST DOCTOR

The wealthiest man in Los Angeles with a medical degree is Dr. Armand Hammer, but don't go to him if you're not feeling good; he hasn't practiced medicine for years. (He is a part owner of Arm & Hammer and might conceivably prescribe a dose of baking soda.) Dr. Hammer, 88, went to Russia from med school, presumably found it more interesting than medicine and entered into various trading deals, and became a good friend of Lenin. He has continued to cultivate his Soviet connections while becoming an industrial giant in the U.S. He is the wealthiest Russophile in the world and probably the most influential. Occidental Petroleum is his. He could probably write a check for about $180 million.

RICHEST SIXTH-GRADE DROPOUT

No L.A. citizen who left school in the sixth grade has ever amassed a fortune to match that of black philanthropist Eula McClaney, 72, a shack-raised child of poverty-stricken Alabama sharecroppers, who heard the Lord say to her, "Save every penny you get and go into real estate." Saving and sacrificing, she bought houses, and lives in a 22-room

French Provincial mansion in Holmby Hills that backs up on singer Neil Diamond's house and is next door to Hugh Hefner's. Honored by the mayor for her philanthropies which run into the megamillions, with an elementary school named after her (the Eula McClaney Christian School), Eula is systematically giving her fortune to charity, paying back the Lord for his goodness.

LARGEST CASKET MAKER

The largest independent maker of coffins on the West Coast is S&S Casket Company of Glendale, which produces coffins in bronze, fiberglass, mahogany, and pine, including all-wooden boxes held together with dowels for Jewish Orthodox, whose religion forbids nails or metal hinges. S&S employs 100 people and turns out 20,000 coffins a year.

MOST EXPENSIVE PRACTICAL JOKE

No practical joke on record was as costly in so many ways as that played on one Beverly Hills rich kid by another. It's all part of a darker story, much told in *Esquire* and newspapers, but the practical joke, if that it was, was played by a young man, Ron Levin, on a man named Joe Hunt, who was his close friend and a partner in many dubious get-rich-quick schemes. Hunt claimed to be a genius in commodity trading. He was short of money at the moment, but told Levin that if Levin would put $5 million into a commodity account at a brokerage house, he, Hunt, would run it up into an enormous fortune which they would split. Levin agreed and Hunt, using the account Levin established for him at the brokerage house, began to make investments. Hunt made good his boast. After weeks of nerve-wracking trading, he parlayed the $5 million into $13 million.

With an $8-million profit, exhausted but triumphant, Hunt asked Levin for his half, $4 million. To Hunt's stunned disbelief, Levin told him there was no $4 million; Levin had never put up a dime. He had told the brokerage firm that he was making a documentary on commodity trading and that the transactions were never to be consummated. Hunt, who thought he had made a fortune, was as broke as the day he started.

Was it done for laughs? No one knows, but Hunt wasn't laughing. A short time later, Levin disappeared and has never been seen again. Hunt has been arrested and charged with his murder. He is asking Hollywood producers $1.5 million for the movie rights.

On April 22, 1987, he was found guilty of first-degree murder.

FIRST PORTABLE STRESS TEST

A Los Angeles clinical psychologist and stress management expert, Alfred A. Barrios, has invented the world's first portable stress indicator.

Easy to carry in a wallet for all potentially stressful occasions, the card is about the size of a credit card and contains a black liquid crystal which reacts with extreme sensitivity to the temperature of fingers placed upon it. If the subject is relaxed, the liquid will be blue; if tense with a skin temperature below 94 degrees, the indicator will change from blue to green to red to black. Black indicates maximum stress. The $3.95 card is selling in the millions.

MOST PUBLICIZED PRINCIPAL

The most famous principal in Los Angeles and, in fact, in the United States is a 45-year-old black man, George McKenna, who is the principal of George Washington Preparatory High School in Southwest Los Angeles. (McKenna added the word *preparatory* to the school's name to give the students the feeling they were, indeed, preparing for something.) His success in turning a violence-ridden substandard high school in the inner city into a model campus first brought him to the attention of President Ronald Reagan, who, in 1984, mentioned him in two speeches and invited him to the White House. In November 1986, he was the subject of a two-hour CBS movie, "The George McKenna Story," which was seen by an estimated 113.5 million households. By 10 A.M. the day after the movie, he had blood on his shirt as the result of stopping a battle between two students.

SMARTEST HIGH SCHOOL IN CALIFORNIA

The smartest high school in the nation is John Marshall High, an inner-city, multi-racial Los Angeles school which in April 1987 defeated nearly 400 students from 38 states to win the U.S. Academic Decathlon. Marshall scored 49,369 points out of a possible 60,000. Marshall is the first non-Texas school to win the decathlon since 1983 when Beverly Hills High won. Three of the Marshall nine-person team were not born in the U.S.

The decathlon was conceived as a way to give bright students some of the competitive glory that comes to athletes. The schools' best and brightest compete in written tests, interviews, speeches, and essays. Subjects covered: economics, fine arts, mathematics, science, literature, and social science.

The victory is considered particularly significant as the competition is usually dominated by highly affluent communities. About half of Marshall's students are from low income neighborhoods.

ONLY TWINS TO MARRY FATHER AND SON

In 1981, Pam Savitt, a beautiful 27-year-old Los Angeles translator, married a young man she met in her apartment house. Two months later, her equally attractive beautiful twin, Pat, a ballet teacher, married the young man's 78-year-old father—history's first instance, it is believed, of twins marrying father and son.

Pat's twin sister is now her daughter-in-law, and Pam's husband is not only her brother-in-law, he is her stepson. If Pam has children, Pat will be their step-grandmother.

MOST "WOMEN-OWNED" BUSINESSES

In no cities in the United States do women own as many businesses as they do in the Los Angeles–Long Beach area. Women of this area own 117,468 businesses, a number far surpassing that of the next closest area, New York–New Jersey (101,223).

MESSIEST STREETS

The worst time of the year for the street-cleaning department is during Los Angeles's annual Street Scene celebration, which honors the city's ethnic diversity. Celebrants create more street trash than accumulates at any other time or place.

MOST COSTLY NEW YEAR'S CUSTOM

Los Angelenos can't wait for the New Year. Millions throw their old calendars out of the windows and into the streets on the day before New Year's. The streets are so littered with calendar pages that cleaning up the clutter is the street-cleaning department's greatest cost for a single day.

The task requires a foreman and 11 workers, backpack blowers, a flusher vehicle, and three huge mechanical sweepers, all working 48 hours.

MOST BOOKS SOLD

In proportion to its population, there are more books sold in Beverly Hills than in any other city in the world. The favorite subjects are sex, gambling, dieting, and show business.

LARGEST DOLL HOUSE COLLECTION

The largest collection of doll houses, miniatures, and toys on the West Coast is found in Santa Monica in a renovated Victorian mansion called Angel House, run for the benefit of developmentally disabled children.

The collection features tiny antique furniture worth hundreds of dollars an item and rare antique doll houses worth up to $25,000.

BIGGEST REPORT CARD ERROR

Although formal records are not kept of the crimes teachers commit marking report cards, certainly a music teacher in Beverly Hills must be high in their infamous ranks. This fortunately anonymous lady gave a D in music to a young music student named André Previn.

AUTHOR READ BY MOST GRADE-SCHOOL CHILDREN

The L.A. author read by more children than any other was Elizabeth Rider Montgomery Julesberg, whose books about Dick, Jane, Sally, Spot, and Puff were first-grade primers for more than twenty million children.

Elizabeth Julesberg was a 42-year-old first-grade teacher in the Los Angeles schools when, appalled at the dullness of the primers and the absence of interesting books, she devised her Dick and Jane stories. The first of her series appeared in 1940, entitled "We Look and See."

Health

LOS ANGELES is known as the city of beautiful bodies, health fads, reducing salons, and gyms of incredible luxury and sophistication. It is the home of Jane Fonda, whose aerobic tapes are the best-selling video tapes in the United States and the most heavily traded tape on the Russian black market. But the fitness of a few does not necessarily reflect the health of the many. The story of Los Angelenos is more complex than the highly visible craze for highly visible fitness. Los Angeles superlatives in the field of health take many surprising turns.

LARGEST HOSPITAL

Admitting 100,000 patients a year and treating almost half a million additional patients in its emergency and outpatient clinics, Los Angeles County USC Medical Center, commonly known as County, is the largest hospital in the Los Angeles area and the largest acute-care hospital in the United States.

Each year, on average, 17,000 babies are born in County—one out of every 217 babies in the United States.

LARGEST SELLER OF UMBILICAL CORDS

Los Angeles County USC Medical Center is the area's largest, and perhaps only, seller of umbilical cords.

When a newborn baby is delivered, the umbilical cord is snipped off, measured, and thrown into a refrigerator. The umbilical cords will later be sold to a medical supply house for 50 cents a foot and used in vein transplant surgery.

Mothers are reported as being pleased to learn that their newly born babies are already helping someone else to a better life.

MOST HOSPITAL MIDWIVES

The most midwives to be found on the staff of any hospital in the Los Angeles area are the 32 midwives at USC–County Women's Hospital, who perform 25 percent of the hospital's deliveries.

MOST WIDELY USED FORM OF BIRTH CONTROL

According to Los Angeles Regional Family Planning Clinic, the most widely used form of birth control in Los Angeles is the pill.

The pill however is dropping in percentage of users. Forms of barrier types of birth control are gaining in favor. There are also ethnic preferences: Latins prefer IUD's; some doctors believe this is because the Latin wives don't want their husbands to know they are practicing birth control. Orientals prefer condoms, no reasons given.

HIGHEST BIRTH RATE

Hispanics have the highest birth rate in the Los Angeles area, with 30.2 births per 1,000 people. Asians are second with a birth rate of 24.1 per thousand. Blacks are third with 20.7 births per thousand. Whites are fourth with 11.1 births per thousand.

MOST LEPROSY

It will come as a shock that a disease as historically feared as leprosy, Hansen's Disease, exists in Los Angeles. But it not only exists, it is increasing: in 1983 L.A. had 36 cases, which dropped to 26 cases in 1984 and almost tripled to 61 cases in 1985. By the beginning of 1986, a total of 372 cases were registered in the city and placed under surveillance.

All leprosy in Los Angeles was brought in by immigrants, but residents have little to fear. Fiction and movies to the contrary, the disease is extremely hard to catch even from direct contact with its victims, and no new cases in Los Angeles are the result of anyone catching it from anyone else.

The largest number of immigrants suffering from leprosy come from Mexico, which is responsible for 51 percent. Other sources are: Vietnam 17 percent, Phillipines 14 percent, Micronesia, Thailand, Cuba, China, and the Carribbean 3 percent each.

FIRST OVUM TRANSFER CLINIC

The first ovum transfer center in the United States to help

infertile women actually give birth is the Memorial Medical Center of Long Beach.

A couple want a baby but the wife—we'll call her Woman A—is infertile or has a genetic defect they don't wish to pass to the baby. The husband's sperm is injected into a woman whom we will call a surrogate mother although she will not bear the child. The surrogate mother returns to the office in five days, during which time the sperm has developed into an ovum. The ovum is painlessly extracted from the surrogate mother, whose role is now over. The ovum is transplanted into the uterus of Woman A, who will then carry the baby to term.

In 109 attempts there have been 11 pregnancies, about the same rate achieved through test-tube fertilization. A second transfer center is opening elsewhere in L.A.

SURGEON PERFORMING MOST OPEN-HEART SURGERY

The most open-heart operations ever performed in the Los Angeles area have been done by Dr. Jerry Kay and his team, which in 1985 completed 1,202 such operations at St. Vincent's Hospital and accounted for more than $28 million in patient revenues.

His medical team consists of four senior surgeons, four assistant surgeons, five anesthesiologists, nine heart-lung technicians, nine physician assistants, six nurse coordinators, and about twenty-five nurses and other medical professionals.

Dr. Kay and his team have since moved to Good Samaritan Hospital, where he expects to break his St. Vincent record.

FIRST PANCREAS TRANSPLANT

The first pancreas transplant ever performed on the West Coast, and one of only about 900 done worldwide, was performed in December 1986, on a 40-year-old Glendale woman suffering from severe diabetes, by Dr. Patrick Soon-Shiong at UCLA. UCLA is one of only four pancreas transplant centers in the United States. At UCLA a pancreas transplant will be performed only on patients who have already had a kidney transplant operation.

ONLY HOSPITAL TO PERFORM FOUR MAJOR TYPES OF TRANSPLANTS

The only hospital in the Los Angeles area, and one of only a very few in the United States, with a center to provide transplant surgery for all four types of major organs is UCLA, which can perform transplants of heart, liver, kidney, and pancreas.

MOST DOCTORS PER CAPITA

The most physicians per capita enjoyed by any city in the world are in Beverly Hills, which boasts 550 medical doctors—one for every 60 residents. This is ten times the national average of one M.D. for every 612 people.

MOST SEX CHANGES

The most sex changes ever experienced by anyone in the Los Angeles area were those undergone by Mrs./Mr. John/Jeanne Moray* of Inglewood.

*Name changed.

When she was 27, and already the mother of two children, a boy and a girl, she felt that, despite her uniquely feminine accomplishments of giving birth twice, she was in fact in the wrong body—a man imprisoned in a woman's body—and 3 months after the birth of her second child, she underwent a sex change which made her a man.

Almost immediately, she felt she had made a mistake and she asked her doctor to try to reverse it. When he refused, she went the other way and took male hormones and grew a beard and in every way became a man, including the possession of a penis.

Her daughter refused to speak to her again, claiming she had killed her mother. After ten years as a man, she felt that her destiny was to be a woman, and she underwent another sex change to restore her womanhood. Thanks to hormones she is beardless once again and has her feminine shape back, but not her daughter. Her son remained loyal during the whole process.

LARGEST SURROGATE MOTHER CENTER

The largest organization in Southern California serving couples wishing to have a child through a surrogate mother is the Center for Surrogate Parenting in Beverly Hills.

The Center charges $30,000, which includes the fee of the surrogate mother, about $10,000. If the surrogate mother is married, her husband must sign an agreement not to have sex with her until she becomes pregnant, which has taken as long as seven months or more.

FIRST UNION FOR SURROGATE MOTHERS

The first union for surrogate mothers in the United States

was Mrs. Alice Kistler of Glendale, who, on October 18, 1956, gave birth to a daughter, Suzan. The mother's age at the time was 57. Although her achievement is contested by a relative who says she changed the birth date, she is immortalized in the *Guinness Book of World Records*.

MOST PSYCHIATRISTS PER CAPITA

The highest concentration of psychiatrists and psychologists in the world is to be found in Beverly Hills, which boasts (if that's the correct word) 250 practicing psychiatrists and 110 psychologists, giving the city one shrink for every 90 9/10 inhabitants. The 9/10 of a person is presumably a split personality. The Beverly Hills shrink-patient ratio is higher than is found in most mental hospitals.

Twenty-two entire states have fewer psychiatrists and psychologists than Beverly Hills. The Beverly Hills practitioners charge the highest fees in the nation, up to $165 an hour. But why not, if the patients are crazy enough to pay it?

L.A.'S MOST DANGEROUS SEX GAME

The most dangerous sex game played in Los Angeles, or perhaps anywhere, is the one which, according to ex-coroner Thomas T. Noguchi, killed actor Albert Dekker. The game is called "autoerotic asphyxia" by psychiatrists. The participant arranges to hang himself, but controls the hanging so that at the very last second, as he is about to lose consciousness, he can release the rope. It is considered by participants to be the ultimate sexual thrill.

The practice, incredibly enough, is apparently so widespread that in Los Angeles County alone there are 20 to 30 deaths a year from autoerotic asphyxia.

MOST HEALTH PROFESSIONALS

The largest concentration of health professionals in Los Angeles is centered in "Bed Pan Alley," the nine blocks of Sunset Boulevard between Hillhurst and Normandie.

Four hospitals: Presbyterian Medical Center, Children's Hospital, Kaiser Permanente, and Edgemont Hospital (Psychiatric) and dozens of nursing homes, pharmacies, and private practices employ an estimated 10,000 doctors, nurses, orderlies, technicians, medical clerks, and other health professionals.

LARGEST IMPORTER OF TIGER BONES

The area's largest importer of tiger bones, as of June 1986, is an Oriental firm in Los Angeles that uses the product in its Sea Horse Genital Tonic Pills. In addition to tiger bone the pills contain, according to the district attorney, antler, deer kidney, and sea horse. The preparation is intended to increase virility and to combat depression.

The tiger bone is imported from China which, with one-fourth of the world's population, should know something about virility.

WORST YEAR FOR HIGH BLOOD PRESSURE

Los Angelenos may not be as laid-back as they seem. Although they are probably the most health conscious people in the United States, the death rate from high blood pressure has been increasing every year. The death rate for the county is 20.3, which is 53 percent higher than the national average of 13.3 deaths per 100,000.

Authorities feel the holistic medicine approach, so popular in Los Angeles, may have backfired: people who think they can control their blood pressure themselves by reducing salt intake, diet, bio-feedback, or medication, may also need medicines which they do not seek.

LARGEST OPERATOR OF NURSING HOMES

The largest operator of nursing homes in the United States, with 93 nursing homes in California, 1,000 nationwide, with 115,000 beds and 1985 revenues of $1.7 billion, is Pasadena-based Beverly Enterprises.

FIRST FROZEN BLOOD BANK

The first private, for-profit frozen blood bank in the Los Angeles area and one of only a half a dozen in the country is HemaCare-Westside, founded in 1986. For people who don't trust conventional blood banks or who want to store their own blood, the agency will freeze their blood to 120 degrees below zero Fahrenheit and store it for up to three years. The cost: $235 to store one pint for three years. Additional pints can be frozen and stored at a lower rate.

LARGEST MEDICAL ASSOCIATION

The Los Angeles County Medical Association with more than 100,000 members is the largest county medical society in the nation.

GREATEST CAUSE OF DEATH

Blamed for the loss of 22,000 lives annually, the prime cause of death in Los Angeles is heart disease. The second killer is cancer with 13,000 deaths. Third come diseases of the respiratory system with 3,800 fatalities.

RACE WITH MOST HIGH BLOOD PRESSURE DEATHS

The highest death rate in Los Angeles County for diseases associated with high blood pressure is that of the black population, which experienced a death rate of 47.7 per 100,000.

Second: Latinos 19.9 deaths per 100,000; third: whites 18.7; fourth: Chinese 17.1; fifth: Japanese 11.16; sixth: Koreans 3.2.

WORST YEAR FOR GONORRHEA

Although popular perception is that the incidence of venereal disease is decreasing, gonorrhea in the United States and in Los Angeles has reached almost epidemic proportions. In the ten-year period from 1976 through 1985, the worst year was 1985, with 60,000 cases reported in Los Angeles in that single year. The age group most affected is 20–24.

YEAR WITH MOST SYPHILIS

Syphilis is on the decrease in Los Angeles, and while not nearly so prevalent as gonorrhea, is still present in significant and surprising numbers for so serious a disease. In the ten-year period 1976 through 1985, the worst year was 1980, with 2,100 cases. Age group most affected, 25–29.

HIGHEST-PAID PARAMEDIC

The highest-paid paramedic in history is believed to be Reynoldo Wilson, a Los Angeles County firefighter who, in 1986, earned $98,483.65.

Wilson's regular pay as a paramedic is $38,810.72. By

working 120 hours a week, he earned $59,672.93 in overtime.

The Fire Chief's salary was $93,079, but he's not eligible for overtime.

FIRST TOOTH TATTOOS

The first people—perhaps in the world—to walk around sporting butterflies, hearts, and girls' names tattooed on their teeth are several hundred customers of a Canoga Park dental ceramist, Daniel Materdomini.

The designs—flags, nudes, or what have you—are tattooed on a cap, dentures, or a veneer for only $50.00, plus dentist's fee. They are very popular with celebrities who want that little something extra in their smiles.

ONLY MAN LEGALLY NAMED GOD

The only man in the Los Angeles area, and perhaps the world, legally entitled to call himself God, is a former disc jockey, Terrill Williams of Palm Springs. God, née Williams, said he had been visited by three extraterrestrials who suggested if he made the change he would be able to do great things for mankind. Three attorneys advised him no judge would grant such a petition. But a judge did decree that since nobody objected, Williams could henceforth be legally known as God.

The name God appears on his driver's license, but the phone company refuses to list it.

Far from helping mankind, God found he had difficulty even getting a job raking leaves. People, it seems, were leery about hiring God.

Nature

NO METROPOLITAN city lives closer to nature than Los Angeles and is more at the mercy of its vagaries. Brush fires, droughts, tides, winds, landslides, earthquakes require her residents to retain at least some spirit of the pioneers. This hilly desert by the sea is also host to a more dazzling variety of flora and fauna, wild and cultivated, than the world offers in any other large city.

TALLEST TREES

The tallest trees in Los Angeles are the eucalyptus. Like most trees which flourish in L.A., the ubiquitous eucalyptus is not a native. The originals were all imported from Australia.

WORST FIRE

The 1961 fire in Bel Air and Brentwood was not only the worst fire in Los Angeles, but it was also the worst fire in California's history and the fifth worst in U.S. history. It destroyed 494 homes and caused $25 million in property damage.

WORST EARTHQUAKE MONTHS

Of the five major earthquakes that have hit Los Angeles in the past 128 years, four of them have occurred in the months of January, February, and March, with two of the four occurring in March.

BIGGEST EARTHQUAKE

The largest earthquake ever to hit Los Angeles occurred on February 9, 1857, and measured 7.9 on the Richter scale. For comparison, the worst earthquake ever to hit anywhere in California, the famous San Francisco earthquake, measured 8.3 on the Richter scale.

WORST QUAKE OF 20TH CENTURY

The worst Los Angeles earthquake of recent times occurred in San Fernando on February 9, 1971, and measured 6.4 on the Richter scale.

SAFEST PLACE TO BE IN AN EARTHQUAKE

According to experts, when that big earthquake they have been promising Los Angeles strikes, the safest place to be will be in one of the new high-rise buildings. Any floor!

MOST EXPENSIVE TREE

The most expensive full-grown tree currently for sale in the Los Angeles area is a palm, a 55-foot-tall Phoenix Reclinata with 18 trunks. The price: $85,000, plus the cost of moving it to its new location.

The tree is for sale by Valley Crest Tree Co., which buys thousands of trees (particularly large ones) each year from private owners and then resells them for approximately ten times the purchase price. The Phoenix Reclinata was purchased from a front yard in Glendale.

MOST EXPENSIVE NATURAL CHRISTMAS TREE

The most expensive natural Christmas tree in L.A. history is a fir bought in 1984 for the Fashion Island Shopping Mall at a cost of $35,000. At 90 feet, the tree, hauled in from Mount Shasta, was 40 feet higher than the White House tree and 15 feet higher than the Rockefeller Center tree. A worker spent 10 days installing 3,000 lights.

MOST NUMEROUS TREES IN LOS ANGELES

The most common tree in the Los Angeles area is the palm. With 48,000 palms, L.A. has more than any other U.S. city, and more than all of Hawaii.

And the palm is not even a native of Los Angeles. But then, who is?

HIGHEST POINT

The highest point in the City of Los Angeles is Mount Lukens, which is 5,047 feet above sea level. The peak is named for Theodore P. Lukens, an early conservationist.

HOTTEST DAY

The hottest day in the history of Los Angeles occurred in 1885 when the temperature reached 106 degrees Fahrenheit.

HIGHEST MINIMUM TEMPERATURE

Each day's temperature is recorded by the National Weather Service listing the highest temperature of the day and the lowest. The highest low temperature ever recorded was reached on August 19, 1986, when the temperature at Los Angeles Civic Center refused to drop below 76 degrees Fahrenheit.

MOST SUMMER SUN

There will be bitter debates over this by jealous chambers of commerce, but Los Angeles has sunshine year-round 73 percent of the time and in the summer has the nation's greatest number of sunny days (except for desert areas and who wants to live there in the summer?). The summer sun shines 83 percent of the time.

HIGHEST WIND SPEED

The fastest wind ever recorded in Los Angeles is 49 miles an hour.

RAINIEST YEAR

The most rainfall ever to hit Los Angeles in a single year occurred in the 12-month period from July 1 to June 30 (the period known as the weather year) in 1883–1884 when 38 inches of rain fell on downtown Los Angeles, more than *two-and-a-half* times Los Angeles's average rainfall of 14.85 inches.

GREATEST ONE-DAY RAINFALL

The most rain which ever fell on Los Angeles in one 24-hour period occurred in 1934 on New Year's Eve. In that single day, the city suffered 7.36 inches of rain, more than one-half the amount of 14.85 inches which normally falls on L.A. in an *entire year*!

MOST VENOMOUS FISH

Animals and fish can be rated poisonous or venomous. A venomous creature has in its body poison that it injects into its victims. The distinction of being the most venomous fish in L.A. waters is shared by two fish: the stingray and the sculpin.

MOST POISONOUS FISH IN L.A. WATERS

The most poisonous fish in L.A. waters is the puffer, an innocuous-looking fish with a square face and kind eyes. But just because he won't eat you, don't you eat him.

MOST DANGEROUS FISH

The most dangerous fish in local waters is the white shark. Just when you thought it was safe to go in the water.

MOST DANGEROUS LIVING THING IN LOS ANGELES WATERS

Fearsome as the white shark may appear, a microscopic creature has killed or disabled far more people. It is the organism that makes up the so-called red tide that turns local waters red and pollutes clams and other shellfish to the point that eating them can cause severe illness or death.

BIGGEST CRITTER IN LOCAL WATERS

The largest creature of any sort that swims in local waters, and certainly one of the most intelligent and good-natured, is a mammal, the blue whale, which can reach 100 feet in length. They are found mostly near Catalina Island. The whales seen nearer the Los Angeles beaches are gray whales, which are a mere 50 feet long.

HEAVIEST FISH

The heaviest fish that swims in the Los Angeles coastal waters is the black sea bass, which weighs in (if you catch him) at an average of 450–500 pounds.

LONGEST-LIVED CRUSTACEAN

The longest-lived crustacean to be found in local waters is the lobster, which can live to be 50 years old.

BRIGHTEST FISH

The brightest fish—in color, not smartness—to be found in Los Angeles coastal waters is the Garabaldi, dyed by nature a bright orange. This spectacular fish is, as might be expected in a state that worships beauty, the official state fish.

LARGEST EXPORTER OF SEA URCHIN ROE

The largest exporter of sea urchin roe is Santa Barbara, which in 1985 took 9.5 million pounds of that delicacy (ugh) from the Santa Barbara Channel and exported it to Japan.

HIGHEST-CALORIE FRUIT

The highest-calorie fruit raised in the kitchen gardens and orchards of Los Angeles is the avocado, which contains 741 calories per edible pound.

LOWEST-CALORIE FRUIT

The lowest-calorie fruit or vegetable raised by L.A. backyard gardeners is the cucumber, which averages 73 calories per edible pound.

LARGEST FLOWER MARKET

The wholesale flower market at 7th and Wall is not only the largest in Southern California, it is also the largest in the western hemisphere. The market opens at 2 A.M. and closes at noon, five days a week.

LARGEST ATRIUM

The largest collection of growing flowers in Los Angeles can be found in the atrium of the downtown Crocker Center, where 4,000 individual plants are maintained in soil no more than 24 inches deep. The flowers are changed every two to three months, endowing the atrium with a seasonal beauty. The cost: $7,000 a month. As someone once said of Rockefeller Center, "It shows what God could do if he had money."

LARGEST PINE CONES

The largest pine cones in the L.A. area are from the Arau Caria Bidwillii, more popularly known as the bunya-bunya tree, and can attain the size of a bowling ball and weigh as much as ten pounds. The bunya-bunyas were imported from Australia about 80 to 100 years ago and planted next to Victorian mansions. Only a few remain: about six in Riverside, a couple at the Arboretum in Arcadia, and a few strays here and there.

GREATEST VARIETY OF STREET TREES

No city maintains a larger variety of trees than Beverly Hills, which has planted 51 different species of trees. These exquisitely groomed trees are planted in rows sometimes miles long, bordering 51 streets, one species to a street.

LARGEST FIG TREE

The largest fig tree in the Los Angeles area and indeed in the whole United States is a Ficus Macrophylla, known as the Moreton Bay fig tree, in Santa Barbara at Capala and Montecito streets. The trunk is 38 feet around, and its branches have a spread of 165 feet—in case anybody gives a fig.

MOST LIVING IMMIGRANTS

Los Angeles, like New York in its melting-pot days, is a city of immigrants, but the greatest number of transplants from abroad occur in its plant population: 98 percent of all plants in Los Angeles were brought here from other countries.

BIGGEST CAUSE OF POWER BLACKOUT

High winds and rain alone are not the greatest cause of power failure. That dubious honor belongs to L.A.'s 160,000 trees whose falling limbs and sheer upward thrust against power lines cause more outages than any other source.

Keeping those 160,000 trees trimmed is essential for power to be maintained. When the city planted most of these 160,000 trees 20 years ago, it never expected them to be the major source of power failures, but they are. The cost of tree trimming is one of the city's highest maintenance expenses, costing $7.9 million for 1984–85.

MOST WILD ANIMALS

No urban area in the United States and perhaps the world is home to so many wild animals as Los Angeles. Along Mulholland Drive and in the foothills of the Santa Monica Mountains, from Griffith Park to the San Diego Freeway, are found:

Coyotes. Hundreds roam freely, into the very city occasionally, lean, mean, anorexic-looking predators who have adapted admirably to their environment. They feed on small animals, occasional pets, and the bounty of carelessly covered garbage cans.

Raccoons. About 30 roam the area, hunting at night very much as the coyote does. They grow to as much as 25 pounds.

Deer. Some 100 to 300 California Mule Deer (named, unkindly, for their mulelike ears) roam the surrounding hills. They attain 150 to 300 pounds, with regular "hat-rack" antlers.

Grey Fox. A small animal (10 to 15 pounds), about 15 live along Mulholland Drive with perhaps another 100 or so in the mountains.

Striped Skunk. About 50 of these cat-sized stinkers live in nearby hills with scores more deep in the mountains.

Bobcat. Forty fighting pounds of cat, these beautiful predators, some within leaping distance of the city, live on small animals.

Virginia Opossum. A few hundred locally and thousands more live in the foothills. Each weighs about ten pounds and eats everything.

California Brush Rabbit. Thousands—well, you know rabbits—found locally, often in city gardens.

MOST DANGEROUS WILD ANIMAL

The most dangerous wild animal in the Los Angeles area is the mountain lion, a.k.a. the puma or cougar.

The Los Angeles mountain lion is one of nature's fiercest creatures, weighing in at up to 200 pounds of fighting fury. While they range mountains within a 50-mile radius of City Hall, mountain lions have been sighted in Beverly Hills, and in Studio City, Tarzana, and Chatsworth. They live on small game—rabbits, possums, rodents—but also prey on cattle and are estimated to dispatch one or two deer a week. They are nocturnal, so no one knows how many live in the hills and valleys around L.A., but a couple of dozen might be a good estimate, give or take a lion or two.

MOST POISONOUS SNAKE

The most venomous snake in the Los Angeles area is also its only poisonous one, a universally misunderstood reptile whose sighting brings but one thought, Kill! He is in fact a dedicated public servant who devotes most of his active time to clearing vast areas of rodents, an unpleasant job which would otherwise have to be performed by the city, less efficiently and at great public expense. He is found in the Hollywood Hills and in Beverly Hills at varying lengths, all frightening, up to one yard. A subspecies of the western rattlesnake, he has the railroadlike name Southern Pacific rattlesnake.

For all his fierce reputation, if given the chance, he will always retreat when confronted by a human being.

LARGEST BIRD

Standing three feet tall and with a wingspread of more than six feet, the largest bird in the Los Angeles area is the Golden Eagle. He dwells in mountains and the hills which define Los Angeles, along Mulholland, up to the western end of the San Fernando Valley. Almost extinct, there are believed to be only six pairs within about a 40-mile radius of L.A. and perhaps 1,000 pairs in all California. They mate for life though in their fight for survival a little promiscuity might be forgiven. This splendid monogamous bird of prey lives on rodents, rabbits, and some birds.

LARGEST WILD ANIMAL SANCTUARY

The largest wild animal sanctuary in the United States is the Wildlife Way Station in Little Tujunga Canyon. On 160 acres director Martine Colette houses at any given time between 600 and 1,000 homeless wild animals, including on a typical day perhaps 100 lions and tigers, dozens of bears, maybe 40 wolves, 25 leopards, 50 mountain lions, a few elephants, and assorted deer, raccoons, coyotes, monkeys, hawks, owls, bobcats, crows, eagles, and foxes. And perhaps a partridge in a pear tree.

Established in 1969 by Ms. Colette, the Way Station takes in wild animals that have been hurt and nurses them back to health. Many are wild animals that were purchased by people who thought them cute as cubs but had no room for them when they were full-grown lions or tigers, which are unlawful to keep in the city. The Way Station has a staff of 22 full-time professionals and numerous volunteers.

LARGEST VARIETY OF BIRDS

With the exception of San Diego County, Los Angeles County has a larger variety of birds of all species (including such exotica as the Yellow Headed Parrot of which there are now thousands) than any other area in the United States.

MOST ENDANGERED BIRD

The most endangered bird in the Los Angeles area is the peregrine falcon. Only six to eight are known to exist in the entire county.

Once plentiful, they fell victim to DDT and other pesticides that fatally thinned their egg shells, and to falconers who kidnapped the young for their sport. But they are coming back. In 1970 the entire state could boast only two pair. The comeback has been led by an L.A. group that raises them in captivity and then releases them. There are now more than 77 pairs statewide.

L.A.'s peregrines live in the Wilshire corridor, nesting in the high-rise buildings and swooping down from the rooftops at incredible speeds to snare pigeons and other small birds in midflight. They are most likely spotted at the La Brea Tar Pits and at the Union Bank Building downtown. They weigh in at about two pounds and have a wingspread of three and a half feet.

MOST BIRDS OF PREY

Only one other spot in the United States, Snake River, is

home to more flying predators than Los Angeles, and no other metropolitan area even comes close. Los Angeles is host to 14 species, including the Red-tailed Hawk, its most populous bird of prey, the Peregrine Falcon, the Great Horned Owl, and the Golden Eagle.

BIGGEST ANIMAL IN ZOO

The biggest animal in the Los Angeles Zoo is an African bull elephant, Samson, who weighs in at five tons.

SMALLEST ANIMAL IN ZOO

The smallest animal at the L.A. Zoo is the Fire Bellied Toad, who tips the scales at two ounces.

LARGEST SELLER OF ANT FARMS

The world's largest vendor of ant farms is Milton Levine, chairman of Uncle Milton Industries in Culver City, who started selling ant farms more than 30 years ago and has ever since reigned as the world's foremost ant tycoon.

The standard ant farm hasn't changed much from the original: it's six-by-nine inches of transparent plastic in a solid frame housing 25 to 30 ants.

The purchaser gets a certificate and the ants are sent separately since they don't have a good shelf life. The ant of choice is *pognomyrmex Californicus*, a worker ant—the kind you see on picnics—that is one of the few ants willing to work in the daytime when the kids can watch. The others dig only by night.

ONLY BUTTERFLY PRESERVE

The only butterfly preserve in the Los Angeles area and one of the few in the entire world is found in the El Segundo Dunes, which is the breeding ground for the almost extinct El Segundo Blue Butterfly.

The dunes are part of Vista del Mar Park, formed from the ghostly wasteland created when 400 upper-middle-class homes were removed from 302 acres in the 1960s to make way for the L.A. Airport's new northern runways.

The airport is trying to get permission to put a golf course in the park, but the Coastal Commission is withholding approval until plans are made for a permanent sanctuary (a few acres) for the El Segundo Blue Butterfly.

MOST EXPENSIVE ZOO ANIMAL TO FEED

The most expensive mouth to feed at the L.A. Zoo is not the elephant's. The elephant, although the largest animal in the zoo, eats relatively cheap types of food.

The most expensive animal to feed is the Bull Great Seal or the Bull Sea Lion. These animals reach a weight of 400 to 500 pounds and eat 12 to 15 pounds of mackerel a day. The mackerel, which is a grade fit for human consumption, is the most expensive food per pound consumed by any zoo animal.

The great cats, lions and tigers, are fed full meals only five times a week. The other two days they get half rations one day and bones the other. Their food is a prepared diet that is purchased commercially in bulk and contains meat, vitamins, and other substances and costs only about 50 cents per pound. A 400-pound lion or tiger will be fed only ten pounds per meal.

LARGEST SOURCE OF OCEAN POLLUTION

The largest source of pollution in the L.A. area, and perhaps the largest on the entire West Coast, is the Los Angeles sewage system, which dumps sewage into Santa Monica Bay in such quantities that DDT and PCBs, both highly toxic, have been found in people who regularly eat fish caught in the bay.

There are no fish on the ocean bottom where the sewage is discharged from gigantic pipes; only huge colonies of worms feed on the sewage.

A lawsuit, now pending, would commit L.A. to spend $2.3 billion on improvements.

LARGEST BRUSH FIRE

The largest brush fire in the Los Angeles area occurred in Chatsworth in 1982 and burned 42,000 acres.

WORST LIBRARY FIRE

The fire that almost destroyed the Los Angeles downtown library in 1986, the work of an arsonist, is the worst library fire in U.S. history and perhaps the most disastrous since a fire destroyed the library at Alexandria.

GREATEST CAUSE OF FIRES

Nature is most often blamed for brush and forest fires, but the chief culprit is careless man and the arsonist. Arson is the number one cause of fires in Los Angeles.

In 1985 the city suffered 5,338 cases of arson for a total loss of more than $52 million. These arson fires resulted in only 249 arrests.

GREATEST AID TO LESSENING FIRE FATALITIES

Although the number of fires in the city is not decreasing, the number of fire-related deaths is. The greatest saver of lives is the smoke alarm, which does not prevent a fire but warns occupants when one occurs.

The smoke alarm is now mandated by Los Angeles for all apartments and hotel rooms and recommended for all private dwellings.

WORST SMALL FIRE

The worst small fire in L.A. occurred on December 11, 1985, in Fowler's Gunshop in Rosemead. The fire resulted in seven injuries and four fatalities.

★
Crime

★

CRIME MAY seem to occupy an inordinately large part of this book, but crime unfortunately is an inordinately large part of life in Los Angeles, always occupying at least a portion of the conscious mind and exacting an inordinate toll in emotional drain and worldly goods.

The problem is that crime *does* pay, particularly in Los Angeles. Not only that, but the hours are good. Criminals here, perhaps seduced by the good weather, now ply their tax-free trade more in the daytime than at night. And the majority don't even make house calls: they rob you right on the street, in daylight. If they are inept, the city will send them away for a refresher course in crime at a cost of $15,000 a year in a prison cell, about the same as the yearly cost to send them to Harvard for an MBA.

MOST DANGEROUS HALF HOUR OF THE YEAR

The most dangerous half hour of the entire year in Los Angeles is that immediately following midnight on New Year's Eve.

Thousands of celebrating people run into the streets and welcome the New Year by firing guns into the air, so many thousands of guns, revolvers, shotguns, sawed-off shotguns, even automatic rifles and Uzis that war veterans say it sounds like a battle zone. A bullet from a service revolver fired straight up can reach a height of almost two miles; returning, it picks up the speed and power of a newly fired bullet.

In 1986 a man was killed in front of his wife, and a 13-year-old boy died, both from a returning bullet. A police helicopter, returning from New Year's Eve patrol, found more than 100 spent bullets in its fuselage. The custom prevails throughout the city, but the greatest concentration is in the inner city, South Central Los Angeles.

HIGHEST-PAID OFFICERS

The highest-paid members of the Los Angeles Police Department are helicopter pilots, who receive pay six steps above their actual rank. Next highest paid are members of the bomb squad, who receive pay four steps above their actual rank.

MOST DANGEROUS POLICE ASSIGNMENT

Although the bomb squad would appear to be the most dangerous job on the police force, the highest percentage of fatalities in relationship to their numbers has been suffered by helicopter pilots; in the last ten years at least ten and perhaps as many as 15 have been killed in the line of duty. However, they were not shot at. All the deaths were the result of pilot error or mechanical failure.

Bomb squad experts, a testament to their incredible skills, had never suffered a fatality until 1985, when two bomb squad members, one a world-famous expert, were killed by a pipe bomb they were attempting to defuse. The bomb was booby-trapped with a smaller bomb concealed from view.

DOG MOST USED FOR DOPE SNIFFING

For the extremely delicate work of sniffing out drugs that may be hidden under hundreds of pounds of luggage and deliberately camouflaged with other odors, the breed of dog most used by the LAPD is the German shepherd.

DOG MOST USED FOR DETECTING BOMBS

The dogs most used by the LAPD for bomb sniffing are also German shepherds.

Detection of explosive devices, ever more important in the age of terrorism, would be impossible without the aid of highly trained dogs who sniff out bombs. The dogs are assigned to bomb squad members who train them, and man and dog are thereafter inseparable. The dogs live in their trainers' homes because their lives depend upon how well the man and dog understand each other.

MOST SPEEDING TICKETS GIVEN BY A SINGLE POLICEMAN

The most speeding tickets ever issued in a given time by any of the 7,000 Los Angeles Police Department officers were given by Motorcycle Officer Kelly S. Klatt, 34, who issued a record 435 traffic citations in 19 days.

Klatt traps speeders with a $950 high-tech radar gun, purchased at his own expense. L.A.'s 320 motorcycle cops (who write more tickets than officers in "black and whites") average 8–10 a day. Klatt writes more than 20.

MOST JAYWALKING TICKETS

The most tickets for jaywalking ever handed out in a given period were issued near the USC campus, where in six hours Kelly S. Klatt—when not nailing speeders—and his partner issued 61 jaywalking tickets.

A ticket for jaywalking must be taken seriously. It costs $10.00. If ignored, a warrant is issued, and the fine goes to $180.

SEX MOST LIKELY TO ATTEMPT SUICIDE

Far more women than men attempt to commit suicide in Los Angeles. In 1985 there were attempts by 1,295 women vs. only 1,051 men.

FAVORITE SUICIDE METHOD: WOMEN

Of the 1,295 attempts to commit suicide by women in 1985, the most common method used was sleeping pills, which accounted for 315 attempts . . . but only 19 successes.

Knives or glass and razors tied for second place with 76 attempts each . . . but no successes. Third place was guns with 58 attempts . . . and 19 successes.

FAVORITE SUICIDE METHOD: MEN

The gun is the method of choice for most suicide-bent Los Angeles men. Of 1,051 suicide attempts in 1985, 185 were by gun... 154 succeeded.

Second, hanging or strangling: 62 attempts... 11 successes. Third, jumping: 30 attempts... 19 successes.

MOST LIKELY TO SUCCEED AT SUICIDE

Although more women than men attempt suicide, men are much more successful at it. Of 1,051 attempts in 1985 by men, 305 resulted in death. But of 1,295 attempts by women, only 116 resulted in death.

AGE OF MOST ADULT SUICIDE ATTEMPTS

The most common age at which Los Angeles men and women attempt suicide is 22–29.

MOST MOVING VIOLATIONS

Drivers in the central district racked up more tickets for moving violations than those in any other part of Los Angeles... amassing 1,385 tickets per 1,000 population.

FEWEST TRAFFIC CITATIONS

Perhaps their local policemen are more affable, but for whatever reason the drivers of the Hollenbeck Division garnered fewer traffic tickets for moving violations (the ones that make your insurance go up) than any other area of the city, only 954 in all of 1985.

MOST COMMON KID CRIME

Juveniles are children from 10 through 17. The largest single category of juvenile crimes in Los Angeles is narcotic offenses. Of 22,177 juvenile arrests in 1985, more than 10 percent, 3,558, were for narcotics.

YOUNGEST MURDERERS

Homicide is far more frequent among very young children than generally believed. In 1985 127 juveniles were arrested for homicide. Of these, 19 (17 boys, 2 girls) were in the 11–14 age bracket. When you ask your kid to mow the lawn, watch out!

AGE OF MOST TEENAGE KILLERS

The age at which most juveniles are arrested for homicide is 17. In 1985 there were 45 arrests of 17-year-old males on suspicion of murder.

YOUNGEST RAPIST

The youngest male ever actually arrested for rape in Los Angeles was a boy ten years old, arrested in 1985.

YOUNGEST FEMALE RAPIST

Rape by a female is perhaps the rarest of all crimes. In all of 1985 no adult female was charged with rape. And only one juvenile; she was 17.

YOUNGEST NARCOTIC VIOLATORS

The youngest children actually arrested in Los Angeles

and charged with narcotics violations were three boys arrested in 1985, all of whom were ten or younger.

YOUNGEST PROSTITUTES

The horrifying statistics of youthful prostitution and related offenses show that in 1985 the youngest offenders were 12 juveniles in the 11–14 bracket: 8 girls and 4 boys.

YOUNGEST PUSHER

The youngest pusher of drugs in Los Angeles history was taken into custody at the Martin Luther King, Jr. Elementary School in October 1986. He was nine years old.

His mother's boyfriend had given him a "baggie" containing $500 worth of rock cocaine. Knowing what it was, he passed it around under the desks and some kids sampled it, requiring hospitalization later. As a result of this incident, the Drug Aware Resistance Education Program was extended from the sixth grade to the fourth, a sad footnote to L.A. that her children, instead of the traditional three R's, must now be taught four: reading, 'riting, 'rithmetic, and rock cocaine.

CRIME MOST COMMITTED BY KIDS UNDER TEN

While narcotics violations are the major juvenile offense, children under ten years old are only occasionally arrested for such offenses. They have their own specialty—burglary. Of 118 Los Angeles children ten or under who were arrested for major offenses, 57 (54 boys, 3 girls) were arrested for burglary.

LARGEST AGE GROUP OF JUVENILE MURDERERS

As children become older, they become more likely to solve their problems with homicide. Figures for homicide arrests, starting with ages ten and under, tend to rise with every age group. Of 127 juveniles charged with homicide in 1985, the greatest number in a single age category, 45 (all male), were 17 years old.

MOST FREQUENTLY COMMITTED CRIME BY JUVENILE GIRLS

Crime patterns for juvenile girls are markedly different from those of boys. The most frequently committed crime by Los Angeles girls ages 10–17 in 1985 was larceny, with 513 arrests.

YOUNGEST COUNTERFEITERS

The youngest suspects arrested for forgery and counterfeiting in 1985 were six children: four boys and two girls ages 10–17. Who says L.A. kids can't read and write?

FASTEST POLICE RESPONSE

The fastest police response to an emergency in the Los Angeles area is that of the Beverly Hills Police Department, which responds sometimes in *seconds*. Average time from receipt of emergency to arrival of officers is three minutes, the nation's fastest.

In the famous Van Cleef & Arpels jewelry store robbery in June 1986, that fast response time worked against them. Alerted by a silent alarm, the police arrived at the store in two minutes, not allowing the frustrated robber time to escape. When the jewel thief saw the police outside, he became frightened and took five hostages. He later shot two hostages in the store, and one hostage was shot by a police sharpshooter who mistook him for the thief.

LARGEST COCAINE BUST

The largest cocaine bust in California history was made by LAPD narcotics officers working with Drug Enforcement Administration agents in Orange County when they arrested 11 men in one swoop and seized 1,784 pounds of cocaine with a street value of almost $500 million.

The second largest bust was made by LAPD officers and federal DEA agents posing as drug dealers after a four-month investigation. They met the suspects in the parking lot of Sears (your financial network) in North Hollywood at Laurel and Victory, and seized cocaine with a street value of $226 million. The two suspects were held on $5-million bail each.

These two cocaine seizures represent more money than the combined income from all other Los Angeles crimes put together. And yet, they represent less than one-tenth of the drugs that flow into Los Angeles in one year.

LARGEST MUNICIPAL AIR FORCE

No municipality in the world and very few countries have an air force equal to that of Los Angeles City/County, which between them fly 47 helicopters. (London is patrolled by three, Kenya's entire air force owns 13, and Libya has 82.)

The City of Los Angeles Police Department operates 15 of those helicopters and in 1985 logged 20,000 hours in an around-the-clock air watch. The helicopters carry one of the world's most powerful searchlights, 500 million candle-watt beamers that can turn midnight into midday. The L.A.

County Sheriff's Department flies 15 whirlybirds, 12-person Kirorskys, used by the military in Korea and Vietnam.

TOUGHEST BEVERLY HILLS POLICE CHIEF

As its first police chief, the 600 citizens of Beverly Hills in 1917 chose an ex-jockey, Charles Blair. His strictness became legend. He ordered his motorcycle patrolmen to gun their motors to assure residents that their homes were being adequately patroled. He fingerprinted every salesman who came into Beverly Hills, and if he felt a visitor was unsuitable, he would put him on one of the famous Red Cars and tell the conductor to keep him aboard until he reached Los Angeles.

Blair also served as fire chief and tax collector.

FEWEST COPS PER SQUARE MILE

Sprawled-out Los Angeles has fewer cops per square mile than any other major city in the United States. Los Angeles averages only 20 percent of the cop concentration of New York City, 27 percent of Chicago's, and 36 percent of San Francisco's.

Los Angeles has not only fewer policemen per square mile, it also has fewer policemen per population than any major U.S. city.

LOST AND FOUND'S MOST TURNED-IN ITEM

The Los Angeles Police Department's Lost and Found Division reports that the item most often turned in by honest citizens is the bicycle.

The runners-up in order are: wallets, purses, glasses, and stereos.

TEN MOST WANTED MEN

The ten most wanted men (and women) in the Los Angeles area, as of January 1985, are:
1. Jimmy Osborne, a nighttime "cat" burglar who victimizes homes in Beverly Hills and Santa Monica, perhaps the most active burglar in Beverly Hills history.
2. John Alexander Riccardi, wanted for murder.
3. M. Khalid Khalifa, child molestation.
4. Maria Jasmine Sorro, credit card forgery and grand theft on such a scale that her bail has been set at half a million dollars.
5. Linda Joyce Birdsone and Dwight Orlando Birdsone, a husband-and-wife team wanted for conspiracy and possession of stolen mail. They have been wanted for so long that others indicted along with them in a scheme to steal welfare and income tax refund checks have already served time and been released on parole.
6. Teobaldo Lopez Villanueva, murder of a police officer.
7. Alan Scott Reading, attempted murder.
8. Charles Wilburn Barr III, mail fraud, wanted since 1974.
9. Robert Gonzales, murder, burglary.
10. Steven Louis Jackson, armed robbery.

LARGEST DISTRICT ATTORNEY'S OFFICE

The Los Angeles County District Attorney's office, with 700 prosecutors, is the largest prosecuting agency of its kind in the United States. When newly elected, District Attorney Ira Reiner estimated it would take him most of the year to meet with his 700 prosecutors, who are scattered in branch offices around the county.

BUILDINGS MOST OFTEN BURNED BY ARSONISTS

The building most often burned by arsonists is the arsonist's own home. Of 1,835 arson fires in 1985, which destroyed $17,203,216 worth of property, most were single-family dwellings, townhouses, or duplexes.

Jimmy Breslin defined arson as the "manufacture of vacant lots." Los Angeles's arsonists manufacture an average of five vacant lots a day.

SINGLE ITEM ARSONISTS BURN MOST

The automobile is burned for profit twice as often as any other kind of property.

As no other people, Los Angelenos love their cars, but that passion cools quickly if the owner happens to need the insurance money, or can't keep up the payments. He then torches his once beloved car.

In 1985 1,377 automobiles were destroyed by arson. And they're only the ones the police found out about.

SUREST WAY TO RECOGNIZE AN ARSONIST

In Los Angeles each year several hundred buildings are torched for which there seems to be no profit motive, and such burnings are the work of pyromanicas who set the fires for the thrill of watching. They are always men and inevitably they stay on the scene when the fire engines arrive, apparently deriving a sexual thrill from their deed. Detectives and firemen look for a man with an erection— the surest sign at a fire of the man who set it.

FIRST CAR EVER STOLEN IN L.A.

The very first car ever stolen in Los Angeles was taken from the front of the Morton Club when the driver went inside for a drink. A celebrating young couple grabbed the car and drove off into the dawn.

The car was a steam-driven four-seater White Motor, manufactured by the White Sewing Machine Company of Cleveland. Newspaper accounts of the theft refer to it as an "expensive automobile, costing more than $2,500." It was soon recovered, not surprising in a time when a car was an oddity and there were so few that this one bore the license number 372.

MOST HONEST DEFENSE CONTRACTOR

Of the four major defense contractors (Litton, TRW, Rockwell International, General Dynamics) in the Los Angeles area, only one (TRW) has not been the subject of criminal indictments or civil lawsuits over defense contracts for the U.S. government.

LARGEST FINE FOR DEFENSE FRAUD

The highest penalty ever levied against a defense contractor in the United States is $15 million for fraud, levied against Litton Industries of Beverly Hills.

The $15 million in fines and restitutions was for defrauding the Pentagon out of $6.3 million by deliberately inflating its costs with forged documents, false material costs, and other methods, from 1975 to 1984.

Of the two executive masterminds, one faces ten years in prison and $15,000 in fines, the other $55,000 in fines and up to 125 years in prison.

LARGEST GATHERING PLACE FOR TRANSVESTITES

By some custom based on no logic and anchored by no landmark, the popular meeting place for transvestites, according to the LAPD, is at Western Avenue and Hollywood Boulevard. No one knows why. Being a transvestite, incidentally, is not a crime.

SAFEST PLACE TO RAISE KIDS

The safest place to raise a child in the Los Angeles area away from the influence of evil companions is West Hollywood, where fewer crimes are committed by juveniles than any other area. In 1985 out of 22,177 juvenile crimes city-wide, West Hollywood saw only 640.

HIGHEST CRIME RATE

The highest crime rate in Los Angeles occurs in the Central Division of the LAPD, which averages 499.2 offenses per 1,000 population. It is also the highest in the category "all arrests," with 335.2 arrests for each 1,000 population.

MOST VIOLENT STREET

The single most violent street in Los Angeles is on Skid Row, an area on 5th Street around Los Angeles Street, known as The Pit.

The Pit is the hub for the 15,000 homeless of Skid Row. It is anchored by two cafes, The Plantation and The Golden Gate, which has sprinklers over the door used to drench the loiterers in the golden doorway. The street has, for a single street, what is believed to be the city's highest rate of drunkenness, prostitution, street robberies, muggings, illegal weapons, assaults, purse-snatchings, narcotics violations, and murders. The police station is around the corner.

MOST EXPENSIVE NEIGHBORHOOD TO PATROL

The area in Los Angeles that attracts the most criminals and is consequently the most expensive to patrol is the Central District. It consists of 4.5 square miles with 85 miles of streets. In 1985 the Los Angeles Police Department spent more than $5.5 million per square mile in that area in a largely futile attempt to maintain law and order, twice that of any other neighborhood and almost 20 times that of the lowest crime area.

HIGHEST POLICE COSTS PER INHABITANT

The LAPD figures its costs not only on a square-mile basis but also on the cost per inhabitant. That cost is highest in the Central District. In 1985 the cost for the 144,157 people of the Central District was $537 per person: more than seven times that of the lowest-cost district.

COMMUNITY WITH LOWEST CRIME COST

The lowest cost per resident to police a community was the $76.00 per person spent on the 265,673 inhabitants of the West Valley in 1985.

MONTHS WITH MOST HOMICIDES

Based on 1985 statistics, you are more likely to be murdered in Los Angeles in February or August. Almost one out of every five homicides, 19.8%, was committed in those two months.

MONTH WITH MOST RAPES

Almost 10 percent (9.7 percent) of all forcible rapes are committed in July.

MONTH WITH MOST BURGLARIES

While most of L.A. is out Christmas shopping, a more energetic portion of the population is out stealing. Of 63,987 home burglaries in 1985, 6,205, almost 10 percent, were committed in December.

Professional thieves in Los Angeles therefore make more house calls than doctors.

MONTH WITH MOST ROBBERIES

Robbers are mostly the type of chaps who come up to you in person with gun or knife and demand money, as opposed to the more stealthy class of criminal who breaks into your house or business. Although they each have a rather snobbish professional disregard for the other, their working habits are equally seasonal and robberies reach their peak in the same month. In 1985 9.6 percent of all robberies were committed in December.

The difference between burglary and robbery is that in order to be convicted of burglary, the criminal must enter a structure with the intent of committing a crime, even if the structure is only a phone booth. Usually you are not at home when a burglary occurs.

A rapist who enters a home to commit rape is guilty also of burglary.

CRIME MOST LIKELY TO BE COMMITTED AGAINST YOU

If you live in Los Angeles long enough, the statistical likelihood is that you will become the victim of some form of major crime, and the most likely is some form of larceny, that is to say, theft.

Los Angeles manages to generate about 297,000 major crimes a year (1985 figures as reported by the LAPD to the FBI). Of these the most common, 126,619 reportable offenses, are larcenies.

MONTH WITH MOST AGGRAVATED ASSAULTS

The worst month for aggravated assault is December, which has 10 percent of all the aggravated assaults, an average of 70 a day in the season of Peace on Earth.

Although all assaults are aggravating, the police define aggravated assault as more than an ordinary fistfight or shoving match. Usually a weapon is employed—a brick, a stick, a pipe. The fists of a professional fighter would be considered a weapon.

LONGEST UNSOLVED MURDER CASE EVER SOLVED

The longest it has ever taken the LAPD to solve a murder is 53 years.

In 1927 a Los Angeles police officer was shot in the course of a robbery. Intensive investigation failed to find the murderer, but there is no statute of limitations on murder and the case stayed on the books. In 1980, 53 years later, a man walked into a police station and confessed to the murder. He said his conscience had been hurting. He was sentenced to life imprisonment, but he was in his seventies at the time of sentencing.

GUN CARRIED BY MOST POLICE

The issue gun, and the one with which LAPD officers are trained, and therefore the one most carried, is a .38 Smith & Wesson.

MOST COVETED GUN

The gun most policemen in Los Angeles would prefer to carry is a 9-mm Baretta, but the LAPD requires special training in the weapon, and currently only about 500 officers out of a 7,000-man force are authorized to carry them.

MOST COMMON MAKE OF POLICE CARS

The most common makes of LAPD black and whites are the Ford LTD and the Chevrolet Crown Victoria, both with standard engines straight from the showroom floor.

MOTORCYCLE MOST USED BY L.A. POLICE

The motorcycle most used by the LAPD is the Kawasaki 1000, with a top speed of about 110 miles per hour.

TOP SPEED OF POLICE CARS

In order to discourage high-speed chases, which have resulted in many deaths, LAPD police cars no longer have souped-up engines. Their top speed is about 110 miles per hour, as opposed to the older cars which could hit 140 miles per hour.

MOST FAMOUS UNSOLVED MURDER

Ask any member of the LAPD which is their most

famous unsolved murder, and they will answer without hesitation, the Black Dahlia.

The Black Dahlia was the romantic name given by newspapers to a beautiful young girl with long black hair (hence the name) whose nude body was found dismembered in the Hollywood Hills. Thousands of clues were followed; all proved empty. The police were and are stymied.

But since the day the Black Dahlia's body was discovered, barely a year goes by without someone confessing to the murder. So far 100 people have walked into police stations and confessed to killing the Black Dahlia. And every one of these 100 confessions has been false. How do the police know the confessions are false? Because there was something unique done to the body, something known only to a few detectives. And not one of the people who confessed to the crime knew what that unique thing was.

Why would someone confess to a murder they had not committed? Because, the police say, they are crazy.

MONTH WITH MOST VEHICLE THEFTS

More vehicles are stolen in December than any other month—perhaps to give as presents.

LARGEST THEFT

In one crime a Los Angeles criminal stole more money than any other man perhaps in history. Take all the property stolen by all the burglars, robbers, car thieves, purse snatchers, shoplifters, bank heisters, jewel thieves, hijackers, and all the other outlaws of the entire city of Los Angeles in an entire year—put it in one pile and then multiply it by five.

The crime was committed by Stanley Goldman, chairman of Equity Founding Corporation, and involved more than $2 *billion* in corporate assets.

Goldman manipulated forged bonds and phony insurance policies to create an apparently successful mutual fund that, on close inspection, vaporized, taking the life savings of thousands with it.

LARGEST PRISON ALUMNI ASSOCIATION

The largest association of ex-prison inmates is believed by police to be the Black Guerrilla Family, which now numbers 200 known members in the South-Central area. About 400 others are still in prison.

The organization which originated in the late 1960s in state prisons was originally political, maintaining that blacks were basically political prisoners. Now the Black Guerrilla Family is involved mostly, say the police, in street crimes, centering on the cocaine trade.

The family recruits its members from among L.A.'s 1,500 black gang members in the prison system, with promises of big bucks in street crime once they get outside.

LARGEST RESTITUTION ORDER

The most money a defendant in a Los Angeles municipal court was ever ordered to pay to a plaintiff was $110,000. The verdict was made against a mother-daughter team, Joan McCarthy and Jennifer Armstrong, convicted of grand theft for failing to pay 13 employees for five months.

They had operated the now-defunct Wilshire Club, which called itself the country's first exclusive club for professional women.

MOST EXPENSIVE CALL GIRLS

Beverly Hills has the area's most expensive call girls, with fees averaging $300 . . . and sometimes as high as $1,000. In surrounding communities these same call girls would average $50.

FIRST PRISONER WAREHOUSE

Complying with an order by the U.S. District Court Judge to reduce the population of its downtown jail from 3,000 to a maximum of 1,800 prisoners, the Los Angeles Board of Supervisors voted, in 1986, to buy for $1.6 million a concrete industrial warehouse across from the Central Jail and convert it into a jail.

SHORTEST TIME NEEDED FOR EXECUTIVES TO BUY DOPE

You're a lawyer or a businessman sitting at your desk in Century City and you feel the need for a fix, cocaine or whatever. Now this is a nondrug-dealing neighborhood, and you have no connections, but according to Los Angeles narcotics officers, you can, if you are streetwise, go out and find someone who will sell you a fix in a minimum of three minutes.

SHORTEST TIME FOR HIGH SCHOOL FIX

Although an energetic executive can get a fix in a minimum of three minutes, a high school sophomore trying for a fix would need more time; he must get into a car and ride, window down, past a street-corner dealer who will throw in a packet of coke for a single 20-dollar bill proffered from the half-open window. Fastest average time from desk to dope: four minutes.

LARGEST GHETTO EMPLOYER

According to police spokesmen, the largest employer in minority areas is the segment of the dope industry that supplies crack, the almost fatally addictive form of cocaine. Crack is an equal-opportunity employer, from young kids to old ladies. This cottage industry provides more jobs than McDonald's and is an easy introduction into the high-paying fruits of crime.

DRUNKEST PERSON

To hold the all-time record for alcohol content in the blood in the Los Angeles area is to compete among giants. Nevertheless the record, set in December 1982, belongs to a 24-year-old woman who was determined by the UCLA Medical School to have a blood-alcohol content of 1,510 mg. per 100 ml. That's more than 18 times the limit at which cops hit you with a drunk driving charge and three times the amount usually fatal. Nevertheless, unaware that she was the all-time champ, she walked out of the hospital in just two days—into history and, incidentally, into the *Guinness Book of World Records*.

MOST REGISTERED SEX OFFENDERS

Of the 63,012 offenders who are registered in California, Los Angeles County has the most—26,118. (Alpine County has none.)

Under a 40-year-old California law, any person convicted of rape, sodomy, lewd and lascivious conduct with children under age 14, child molestation, felony exposure, or penetration with a foreign object, and persons who have been declared mentally disordered sex offenders must register with the police in the city in which they live.

When they register, they sign a form stating: "I have been notified of my requirement to register as a convicted sex offender pursuant to Sections 290–290.5 of the California Penal Code. I understand that: I must register within 14 days of coming into any county or city in which I am domiciled with the law enforcement agency having jurisdiction over my place of residence. I must upon changing my residence inform in writing within 10 days the law enforcement agency with which I last registered."

Police estimate that only half of the sex offenders required to register do so.

LARGEST SALES TAX CHEATERS

Since a sales tax was imposed more than 50 years ago, retail store owners have sometimes underreported sales and kept the sales taxes their customers have already paid, but no store owner has ever defrauded the state on the magnitude of Charles Nathan Shooster and his wife, Sonya, of Beverly Hills. According to city attorney James Hahn, the Shoosters, former owners of a chain of gas stations, underreported their sales by $34 million and owe the state $3.3 million in taxes, interest, and penalties.

LONGEST SLUMLORD JAIL SENTENCE

For eluding authorities and tenants for years by using a false name to hide his ownership in slum properties and to evade more that 40 judgments won by tenants for false eviction and unlawful seizures of property, slumlord Nathaniel Wells received the stiffest sentence ever imposed on a Los Angeles landlord: a $9,000 fine and four years in prison, every year of which he served.

In 1986 Wells was again in court, charged with confiscating a tenant's property, including all the children's clothes, while he ran his evil empire from his jail cell.

MURDERED MOST WOMEN

In 1977 and 1978 women of the Los Angeles area were terrorized by a man termed the Hillside Strangler. The bodies of ten women were found strangled in that two-year period. Finally Kenneth Bianchi was arrested and eventually pleaded guilty to five of the murders. He was given six years to life.

His cousin, Angelo Buono, Jr., was charged with assisting him in his slaughter and was charged with ten counts of murder. After a two-year trial, he was found guilty and received a life sentence. The details are still unclear, but one of them, or the two of them in concert, murdered more women than any other man in Los Angeles history.

HIGHEST COUNTY MURDER RATE

The highest murder rate in the ten years 1976–1985 in Los Angeles County occurred in 1980, when the murder rate was approximately 24 murders per 100,000 population.

LARGEST KIDNAP RANSOM

In April 1967, Herbert Young, president of the Gibraltar Finance Corporation, paid $250,000 for the return of his 11-year-old son, Kenneth. This is the largest amount ever paid for the safe return of a kidnapped child.

The kidnapper, a former intelligence agent for the IRS, was caught and sentenced to 20 years to life.

LARGEST REWARD

The largest reward the City of Los Angeles is permitted to offer for the capture of a criminal is $25,000.

MODEL CAR MOST OFTEN STOLEN

Whether or not it can be considered a compliment to the car no one is sure, but one model far outpaces the others in the number stolen—the Toyota Celica. Between 1976 and 1985, 1,466 Celicas were stolen in the Los Angeles area.

This puts it far ahead of the second-place favorite of thieves, who stole 965 Toyota Corollas in the same time period. Third is the Datsun 210, with 915 thefts.

In the previous decade the Volkswagen Bug led the heist parade with 1,624 cars stolen.

Only two American cars have been deemed worth stealing in any quantity. From 1966 to 1975, Ford's Mustang was represented with 944 thefts, and in the following decade the Chevrolet made the "most wanted list" with 768 thefts.

Nationally the most stolen car is the Buick Riviera.

MOST DANGEROUS PLACE TO LIVE IN L.A. COUNTY

The most dangerous place to live in Los Angeles County (as opposed to living in Los Angeles itself) is the Lennox area, which in 1984 had 34 murders and 1,196 assaults.

The second most dangerous place is East L.A., with 30 murders and 1,031 assaults. Third is Lynnwood, with 27 murders and 1,038 assaults.

WEATHER IN WHICH YOUR CAR IS MOST LIKELY TO BE STOLEN

On the average day within the borders of metropolitan Los Angeles, 133 cars will be stolen (235 in L.A. County). This number will rise on rainy days. The rainier the day, the more cars will be stolen.

Apparently, say police experts, some folks would rather steal a car than walk around wet.

NEIGHBORHOOD WITH MOST MURDERS

South Los Angeles (the 77th Police Division) from Vernon Avenue through Century Boulevard, had, in 1983, the most murders of any section of the City of Los Angeles: 123 murders, more than two a week. Runners-up: Silver Lake–Rampart–Echo Park, 84 murders; Southeast Watts, 77 murders; Southwest Crenshaw, 65 murders; Wilshire District, 44 murders; Fairfax, 44 murders; Hollywood, 44 murders; San Fernando–Foothill, 39 murders.

MOST GANG KILLINGS

The bloodiest gang warfare in Los Angeles history as measured in killings occurred in 1980, when gangs were responsible for 192 murders. The second worst year was 1986, with but one fewer killing.

BEST-KNOWN SHOPLIFTER

The most famous person ever to be arrested and accused for shoplifting is Judy Garland, who was arrested for that offense in Beverly Hills.

No city, for its size, boasts as many celebrity shoplifters as Beverly Hills. Other stars who have been arrested and charged with shoplifting include Hedy Lamarr, Veronica Lake, and Louise Lasser.

Quite a few rich folk other than stars don't bother to either charge or pay cash. Each year their taking ways cost those exclusive Beverly Hills stores $3.5 million.

BANK ROBBERY CAPITAL

Since 1969 not one day has gone by without an L.A. bank being robbed, making Los Angeles the bank robbery capital of the world.

Why does L.A. have so many bank robberies? When master bank robber Willie Sutton was asked why he robbed banks, he answered, "Because that's where the money is!" This would hardly hold for Los Angeles; the year's crop of bank robberies in 1985 averaged a pathetic $1,856 per bank holdup.

MOST ROBBERIES: BANKS VS. LIQUOR STORES

Los Angeles is believed to be the only city in the nation where the number of banks robbed exceeds the number of liquor stores robbed. In 1986 418 banks were robbed vs. 351 liquor stores. Perhaps it's because banks take your picture.

BUSINESS MOST LIKELY TO BE ROBBED

By a margin of more than 2 to 1, the business most likely to be robbed in Los Angeles is a café or bar. In 1985, an average year, 1,695 bars and cafés were robbed compared to the runner-up, 714 markets.

BEST THING TO STEAL

If you must steal, LAPD statistics would indicate that the most profitable thing to steal is money.

Money, because it is virtually impossible to identify, has the lowest recovery rate of anything taken. In 1985, of more than $31 million in cash that had been stolen, the owners recovered only $2.5 million.

WHAT BURGLARS STEAL MOST

A Los Angeles burglar would rather steal your jewelry than any of your other possessions; in 1985 it was the most stolen item in the city, with almost $55 million worth of jewelry taken.

Not only is jewelry small and easy to handle (although those greedy fences give the burglar only a fraction of its worth), it's also the item, other than cash, least likely to be recovered by the victim. Of the $55 million stolen, only slightly more than $4¾ million was ever recovered.

STOLEN PROPERTY MOST OFTEN RECOVERED

Of all property stolen in Los Angeles, the most frequently recovered is the automobile. In 1985, of more than $166 million worth of cars stolen, $142 million worth were recovered.

DUMBEST CAR THIEF

On April 18, 1984, a thief stole Mayor Tom Bradley's car from the driveway of the mayor's mansion in Hancock Park. The car, a 1975 Buick Electra, was eventually recovered.

LARGEST LAND SWINDLE

The largest land swindle in American history was masterminded by a Manhattan Beach man, Bernard Whitney, 65, assisted by a Dutch partner. Between 1977 and 1981 they bilked thousands of Europeans out of millions of dollars by selling them acres of worthless land in various U.S. deserts, often land they didn't even own.

LONGEST TIME A CONVICTED FELON HAS PUT OFF GOING TO JAIL

Five years after he was convicted (at age 80) of stealing $8.9 million from one of his companies, C. Arnhold Smith had, as of November 1984, yet to serve one day in jail. His sentence for embezzling $8.9 million may also be a record—one year.

MOST IMMORTAL CON MAN

The most successful con man in L.A. history was a charlatan who professed to be able to cure virtually any illness that flesh was heir to by "magnetizing the iron in the blood."

During the 1920s he marketed a horse collarlike device consisting of two coils of insulated wire and a small bulb that lit up when the device was plugged in. The electricity was supposed to continue on through the body and effect the miracle cure. The medicine man made millions, which he invested mostly in Beverly Hills real estate.

It is this man, H. Gaylord Wilshire, who gave his name to Los Angeles's most magnificent thoroughfare, Wilshire Boulevard.

MOST WANTED WAR CRIMINAL

Los Angeles (Seal Beach) had the dubious distinction of being the home of Andrja Artukovic, an 85-year-old Croatian exile, accused by Yugoslavian officials of complicity in the execution of 770,000 Serbians and Jews during World War II.

"He was," says the former Chief of the Office of Special Investigations of the Justice Department, "probably the highest-ranking war criminal at large in the world today."

After years of legal delay, Artukovic was finally deported to Yugoslavia to stand trial for his alleged war crimes.

MOST DANGEROUS BUS STOP

According to a survey of 1,088 RTD passengers, the one bus stop in all of Los Angeles at which they are most likely to be robbed or assaulted is the one at Hollywood Boulevard and Western Avenue. And at the same corner are committed Hollywood's greatest number of crimes against the bus drivers themselves.

LONGEST SENTENCE FOR GYPSY CAB DRIVER

Gypsy cab drivers are those who operate without a city license. Of 180 prosecutions of gypsy cab drivers, the longest sentence given was to Robert Bonseigneur, 32, who was picked up for operating at Los Angeles International Airport and sentenced to 15 months in County Jail.

VEHICLE LEAST STOLEN

The vehicles least often stolen in Los Angeles are the motor scooter and the bicycle, accounting for only one-tenth of one percent of vehicles stolen.

MOST COMMON AGE FOR COPS

The police officer who responds to your call for help or who gives you a ticket is most likely to be 39 years old. LAPD has more officers in that age bracket than in any other.

OLDEST POLICE ROOKIE

The oldest man ever to join the Los Angeles Police Department is Lewis Ellis, a college-educated black man who became a policeman at age 53.

He had been a part-time reserve police officer from 1972 to 1980, but he wanted to serve full-time. His graduation at age 53 from the Police Academy in 1985 attracted national attention. Five months later he resigned, charging harassment by white officers.

OLDEST POLICE OFFICER

There is no mandatory retirement age for Los Angeles police officers. The oldest officer on active duty is third-class detective John S. John, who is 69 years old.

OLDEST FEMALE POLICE OFFICER

The oldest female currently on active duty with the LAPD is Darlene Sampson, who is 50 years old.

BEST-DRESSED POLICE OFFICERS

According to the National Association of Uniform Manufacturers and Distributers, the officers of the LAPD are the best dressed in the United States. They won the title in a competition against the uniforms of thousands of city, county, and state law-enforcement agencies.

The LAPD uniform is blue serge with long sleeves and is much admired by the officers because it is distinctive, identifying them as officers without requiring them to wear shoulder patches, is trim, easy to keep up, and hard to see in the dark, an important factor in avoiding unsightly bullet holes.

MINIMUM HEIGHT FOR POLICE

After considerable debate, minimum height requirements for men and women of the Los Angeles Police Department are the same: neither can be less than five feet tall.

There are no specific weight requirements, but regulations state that a police officer's weight must be proportional to his/her height.

MAXIMUM HEIGHT FOR POLICE

No Los Angeles police officer may be taller than 6 feet 7 inches—perhaps because they'd make too good a target.

GREATEST DENSITY OF POLICE OFFICERS

The greatest concentration of police in the city is in the Hollywood Division, with 307 officers.

MINIMUM UNPAID TICKETS TO QUALIFY FOR "DENVER BOOT"

If you are a scofflaw who doesn't pay traffic tickets, the minimum number of unpaid tickets you need to qualify to have your car immobilized by the dreaded Denver boot is five.

The Denver boot, new to L.A., is a hellish heavy, metal

device which is locked to the front wheel of your car by a police officer, making it absolutely impossible to move the car. In the last three years motorists have ignored 95,000 parking tickets worth $35 million in fines. Now the police are sending teams around the city with lists of scofflaws, and their cars will get the boot even if legally parked.

NUMBER OF PARKING TICKETS

Every day of 1984 Los Angeles police handed out approximately 4,000 tickets for parking violations to set an all-time city record of 1.4 million parking citations and $25 million in fines in a single year.

However, the city claims it has been too lax; under a new policy it hopes to double the number of tickets to 8,219 a day (3 million a year) and the revenue to $50 million, making your chance of getting a ticket better than your chance of winning the California lottery.

AREA WITH FEWEST MURDERS

The most murder-free section of Los Angeles is Devonshire, which, in 1985, had only nine-tenths of a percent of the city's homicides. Legend has it the area is so peaceful that if an atom bomb were to land, it would just lie there and grow.

WHERE ANGELENOS ARE MOST OFTEN ROBBED

Los Angelenos are more likely to be robbed in the street than in any other place. Of 27,843 robberies in 1985, 17,197 of the victims were pedestrians.

MOST PROSTITUTES

The center of prostitution in the Los Angeles area is Hollywood, where, according to police, nearly 5,000 prostitutes ply their ancient profession.

LARGEST COUNTERFEIT ARREST

The largest amount of counterfeit money ever found in the United States was seized in Buena Park (home of Knotts Berry Farm) in 1987. The sum: $17.7 million, all in $100 bills.

The $100 bills were the work of two men, Harold Cooper, 56, of Buena Park, a cement worker, and Wick Heimandollar, 40, of Salmon, Idaho, a bartender.

The cement worker and the bartender worked together for eight years to perfect an undetectable $100 bill, and their final product would have fooled almost anyone. They made, in fact, only one error; in trying to wholesale $3 million worth of the bills, they chose two undercover Secret Service men as buyers.

★

The City

★

P EOPLE COMPLAIN that Los Angeles isn't really a city, simply a necklace of neighborhoods. It's true her 2,800,000 inhabitants are scattered among 465 square miles, and we find only 6,020 people in a square mile, which is the lowest population density of any major city in the nation.

Los Angeles is surrounded by 100 smaller communities, eight of which have populations of more than 100,000. It is a center, a heart, a sun. If it lacks the vertical crush of population which to some people characterizes a city, it has the great structures, the museums, the centers of learning, the repositories of culture, the parks, the playgrounds, the homes, and the magnets of diversity which say "city" in the most meaningful sense.

SUPERMARKET WITH LOWEST PRICES

Price wars fought by Los Angeles's supermarkets are the fiercest in the nation, with huge ads placed daily in which each chain claims the lowest prices. To help confused consumers, the California Public Interest Research Group, a nonprofit organization, in October 1986 conducted an in-depth price survey of the eight major chains. Volunteer shoppers visited three stores of each chain and purchased 134 items most commonly used. The results were conclusive: the cheapest supermarket chain is Lucky.

SUPERMARKET WITH HIGHEST PRICES

The Public Interest group survey cited above showed that the supermarket chain with the highest prices is Safeway. A shopping cart of groceries that cost $100 at Lucky would cost $110.84 at Safeway. In a year if you bought that $100 basket of groceries at Safeway each week instead of at Lucky, you would pay an extra $536.68.

SUPERMARKET WITH HIGHEST MEAT PRICES

Shoppers who seem perennially shocked at high meat prices might be even more shocked at the discrepancy between markets. The highest-priced meat is found at Hughes Market. Meat that costs $100 at Lucky costs $123.69 at Hughes Markets. Trim and quality are not taken into consideration.

SUPERMARKET WITH HIGHEST PRODUCE PRICES

No item sold in supermarkets varies as much from chain to chain as produce. The chain with the highest-priced produce is Boys. Produce that costs $100.00 at Lucky costs $126.73 at Boys.

HIGHEST-PRICED VEGETABLE SOLD IN A SUPERMARKET

The most expensive single item ever sold in a supermarket produce department is offered by Safeway in West Hollywood—dried white truffles at $200 a pound. Shoppers on a tighter budget may prefer dried morels (mushrooms) for only $199.00 a pound.

MOST PURCHASED ITEM IN SUPERMARKETS

The single item purchased in supermarkets by more Los Angeles shoppers than any other item is bread. Bread shows up in 95.8 percent of all shopping carts.

FIRST WATER BAR

A Rodeo Drive boutique in Beverly Hills has opened the world's first water bar, offering 51 varieties of bottled water. "On the rocks" is a no-no. The bottles are already as decently chilled as a civilized man could wish. Ice cubes would "void out the subtleties." The water, subtleties and all, sells from $1 to $2 a glass.

LARGEST LOBBY

The largest lobby in Los Angeles is the departure lobby of the Tom Bradley Terminal, particularly when you're running for a plane. The first flight of the Wright Brothers would not have made it from wall to wall. The lobby stretches over an expanse long enough to contain easily three football fields.

MINIMUM LEGAL SIZE FOR BEDROOM

Yes, the city is looking into the bedroom. A city ordinance, passed after much debate, decrees that the smallest bedroom permitted for two persons in Los Angeles must by no less than 70 square feet, which would be a room 7 feet by 10 feet. For each additional person another 50 square feet (5 feet by 10 feet) is required. The law is aimed at overcrowding, which often sees two dozen people living in tiny two-bedroom apartments.

MOST DOGS ALLOWED PER HOUSEHOLD

The maximum number of dogs permitted in any one household in Los Angeles is three.

The maximum number of cats per household and the maximum number of birds per household is also three. However, you can have three of each: three dogs, three cats, and three birds.

GREATEST CONCENTRATION OF HOTEL ROOMS

The greatest concentration of Los Angeles's 70,000 hotel rooms is found near the Los Angeles International Airport, an area which offers 15,000 rooms.

FIRST STORE SELLING ONLY KALEIDOSCOPES

The first and so far the only store in the United States selling nothing but kaleidoscopes is Kaleido, in West Los

Angeles, which has selections ranging in price from $15.00 to $1,000.

OLDEST MINIATURE GOLF COURSE

The oldest miniature golf course in Southern California is Shady Acres Miniature Golf in Long Beach.

Miniature golf started in the East in the early 1920s. Shady Acres, built in 1929, is the imaginative creation of Arthur Looff, who with his father also designed some of the world's most beautiful carousels. The Long Beach course features mysteriously disappearing balls, a hand-painted playing card fence, and a tall stone fireplace where golfers warm their hands on a cold night.

LARGEST WATER SPORTS PLAYGROUND

The largest inland water sports area in Los Angeles County is the 3,000-acre Castaic Lake complex, site of most of the boating events of the 1984 Summer Olympics.

Castaic Lake is actually two lakes built in 1971 as part of the California State Water Project. The big lake, behind a nearly mile-long dam, stores water brought 400 miles from the San Joaquin–Sacramento Delta. The earth-fill dam is 5,200 feet long and 335 feet high, half the height of the Hoover Dam.

The lake sends out fingers of 2,630 acres of water with a 35-mile shoreline. One finger of the lake is reserved for water skiing and is stocked with bass, trout, and catfish. A smaller, shallower 150-acre finger is also stocked with fish and used for sail, row, or paddle boats, and swimming.

PORT WITH HIGHEST INCOME

The Port of Los Angeles, a 7,400-acre facility accommodating ships from 70 nations, has a higher net income than any other port in the United States.

PORT ADMITTING MOST FOREIGN CARS

Since cars manufactured in the Orient are more popular than those from Europe, Los Angeles is now the port of entry for more imported cars than any other city in the United States.

LARGEST INSPECTION FACILITIES

The federal facility for inspecting arriving passengers and goods at the Tom Bradley Terminal of the Los Angeles International Airport is the largest such facility in the United States. The 125,000-square-foot facility can process 2,600 passengers an hour.

FIRST SKYSCRAPER

The 27-story Los Angeles City Hall, built in 1926, was the city's first skyscraper. It towered above neighboring buildings, which for reasons of earthquake safety were restricted to 13 stories. The intrepid politicians chose to risk death by earthquake erecting this magnificent edifice for themselves. The city hall remained the tallest building until 1957, when the 13-story limit was abolished.

LARGEST RESTAURANT

The largest restaurant in Los Angeles is an Italian restaurant in the very heart of Chinatown, Little Joe's, which seats

500 guests. Little Joe's was there first, and Chinatown grew up around it.

ALL-TIME CHEAPEST FARE TO LOS ANGELES

The cheapest fare ever to Los Angeles was offered in 1886. You could take your choice of two railroads and ride from St. Louis to Los Angeles for one dollar.

The buck fare was a result of a price war between two deadly rivals, Santa Fe and Southern Pacific. The regular fare in 1885 from St. Louis to Los Angeles was $125. The railroads kept undercutting prices until on March 6, 1886, both railroads dropped their fare to $1.00.

Within a year 120,000 "railroad immigrants" had arrived in L.A. on Southern Pacific alone.

FIRST MOVIE-THEMED PARKING GARAGE

To help drivers remember where they parked their cars in the 9-level garage at the 26-story Century City North office tower, the state's first movie-themed audiovisual aid has been installed. Each floor has a movie as its theme. Drivers are surrounded by music and posters from the movie. When you're met with posters of the Scarecrow and the Cowardly Lion and hear "Over the Rainbow" and "We're Off to See the Wizard," it should be easy to remember you're on the *Wizard of Oz* floor.

TALLEST BUILDING

The tallest building in Los Angeles is the 62-story First Interstate Bank Building at 707 Wilshire. It is 858 feet high and was built in 1974. Runners-up are: Security Pacific Bank Building, 233 S. Hope St., 55 stories, 738 feet;

Atlantic Richfield Building, 515 S. Flower St., 52 stories, 669 feet.

FASTEST ROLLER COASTER

The fastest roller coaster in the Los Angeles area is the Six Flags Magic Mountain's Colossus, a dual-track wooden roller coaster that starts with a first drop of 115 feet and attains a G-force of 3.2 and a speed of 62 miles per hour.

FIRST STAND-UP ROLLER COASTER

The first roller coaster in the world with standing room only is Shock Wave at Six Flags Magic Mountain in which the riders stand through the entire experience. The coaster, all passengers standing, climbs a 90-foot hill, then drops at a speed of 55 miles per hour to enter what the park claims is the single most terrifying moment in thrill ride history: the standing passengers are whipped through a seven-story-high 360-degree vertical loop.

SHORTEST STREET

The shortest street in Los Angeles was once one of its most prestigious addresses. Surrounded by old, well-preserved mansions that border a tiny landscaped park, the shortest street is Pomery Place.

LONGEST STREET

The longest street in Los Angeles is Sepulveda Boulevard, which runs 29½ miles. Runners-up are: Figueroa, 28¼ miles; Mulholland Drive, 23½ miles; Sunset Boulevard, 20 miles; Western 19.7 miles; Vermont, 19.02 miles.

LARGEST EPISCOPAL DIOCESE

The largest Episcopal diocese in the United States is the Los Angeles diocese with 150 churches and 90,000 members.

LARGEST HOTEL

The largest hotel in the Los Angeles area, indeed in all Southern California, is the $180-million, 1,600-room Anaheim Hilton in Anaheim, near Disneyland.

The hotel has two $800-a-night presidential suites and so many meeting rooms that a company could hold a conference a week for a full year and never use the same conference room twice. Its two ballrooms could together act as a hangar for four DC-10s.

The hotel is also Southern California's most empty. Each night (as of February 1985), half the 1,579 guest rooms in the 14-story structure have been unoccupied.

LARGEST INTERURBAN TRANSIT SYSTEM

In 1911 the Pacific Electric Interurban System, with its famous Red Cars, was the largest interurban transit system in the United States, with 60 miles of track linking Los Angeles with the sea resorts along the Pacific coast.

The original purpose of the founders of the line was to sell land along its right-of-way. Some say the line was allowed to die when it had served this purpose. Others say that the oil companies bought it up through dummy companies and then discontinued it so people would be forced to use their cars and therefore consume more gas.

LARGEST CORPORATION

The largest company with headquarters in Los Angeles and the second largest company in the United States is Atlantic Richfield, with annual sales of $26,990 million. Second in Los Angeles is Occidental Petroleum, with $18,020 million in annual sales.

LARGEST ADOBE BUILDING

The largest adobe building in the United States is Mission San Fernando in Mission Hills. Built in 1797, the mission had four-foot-thick walls composed of adobe bricks made of earth mixed with water. The mission complex included stables, granaries, workshops, and houses. It attracted so many Indian converts that for years its population was larger than the population of the then "pueblo of Los Angeles."

The buildings were almost destroyed by vandals searching for fabled treasures believed hidden by the early missionaries, and the walls themselves eventually began to crumble under the California rains. In 1900 a restoration program was begun. The original convent buildings remain, but the 1971 earthquake destroyed the mission church and an exact replica was subsequently built.

LARGEST SPANISH NEWSPAPER

The largest Spanish-language newspaper in the United States, with a daily circulation of 70,000, is Los Angeles's 60-year-old *La Opinion*.

LARGEST AIR FREIGHT COMPANY

The Los Angeles-based Flying Tigers is the world's largest air freight company.

BIGGEST AIRPLANE

The largest airplane ever built in the Los Angeles area, or even to this day anywhere in the world, is the Spruce Goose, originally named "Hercules" by its creator, billionaire Howard Hughes.

The flying boat has eight engines, weighs 190 tons, and is 219 feet long with a wingspan of 320 feet. The aircraft flew only once. Piloted by Hughes himself, it flew 1,000 yards at an altitude of 70 feet off Long Beach on November 2, 1947. The aircraft is now on display in Long Beach.

LARGEST CAR DEALERSHIP

The largest car dealership in the Los Angeles metropolitan area is Longo Toyota of El Monte, which achieved sales of 13,223 new cars in the first ten months of 1984.

LARGEST FLEET OF YACHTS FOR CHARTER

The largest fleet of yachts for charter is managed by Charter Concepts, 13757 Fiji Way in Marina del Rey, which has 40 motor yachts and sailboats available for rental.

LARGEST EDITION OF LOS ANGELES *TIMES*

The largest edition of a newspaper ever published in the Los Angeles area is the Orange County edition of the Los Angeles Sunday *Times* of April 15, 1984 (the Olympic year). It was so swollen with ads that it exceeded the Los Angeles edition of the same paper by 70 pages.

Just carrying the paper home could have been an Olympic event: it contained 856 pages.

LONGEST RAILROAD TUNNEL

The 1.5-mile railroad tunnel in the Santa Susana Pass, built in 1904, was at that time the largest railroad tunnel in the Western Hemisphere. It is still used today.

LARGEST STREET SYSTEM

Los Angeles has the largest street system in the United States. It requires 1,500 workers and $75 million each year to maintain its record-breaking 7,600 miles of streets.

ONLY LAKE TO CATCH FIRE

The only body of water ever to catch fire in Los Angeles is Echo Park Lake. In the oil boom in 1907, so much oil spilled into the lake from surrounding storage tanks that the lake caught fire and burned for three days.

MOST POTHOLES FILLED IN A YEAR

The most potholes ever filled by the Department of Streets in Los Angeles in a single year was 148,375 in 1985. The city encourages drivers to call in and report those pesky spring-breakers, but most people claim the city never fills them anyhow; it just moves them around so you can't memorize where they are.

WORLD'S HIGHEST DAM

The Pacoima Dam, four miles north of San Fernando, was, when erected in 1929, the tallest dam in the world. It is 327 feet high.

LARGEST ARTIFICIAL EARTHQUAKE

The Museum of Science and Industry created a living room that can produce the world's largest artificial earthquake. The room, open to the public, holds 20 people who sit and watch the TV news. Suddenly the anchorman interrupts to say in a horrified voice a big earthquake has hit Los Angeles. The room begins a dance of death simulating a real earthquake.

The museum claims that the temblor is the equivalent of the big one Los Angeles is expecting, 8.3 on the Richter scale. However, scientists say the artificial earthquake is, in fact, about 5 to 6 on the Richter scale. An 8.3 would be 1,000 times as powerful.

The room is part of a comprehensive earthquake exhibit, the largest in the United States.

BIGGEST POLLUTER

The largest commercial polluter of Santa Monica Bay is Chevron U.S.A., which emits more toxic chemical pollutants into the bay than any other industry.

Chevron, abiding by emission standards, is the largest polluter because it is by far the largest refinery in the area. Chevron was the largest contributor, footing 65 percent of the bill, to a fund to work against a state proposition calling for fines on companies which release cancer-causing chemicals into water supplies. Nevertheless the proposition won.

LONGEST MURAL

Ten years so far in the creation, and still unfinished, the longest mural in the world is *The Great Wall*, painted on the side of a flood-control reservoir in Studio City.

The mural measures slightly less than half a mile (2,435 feet) in length and 13 feet in height and will have another 350 to 700 feet added by completion.

Created by young minority artists, it depicts the misfortunes and triumphs of blacks, Asians, Hispanics, Jews, Indians, and other immigrants to Los Angeles who were the victims of severe discrimination.

It starts at the conjunction of Coldwater Canyon and Burbank boulevards.

LARGEST MAN-MADE HARBOR

The Port of Los Angeles, along with the Port of Long Beach to its east, handle between them 125,000 tons of cargo a day and comprise the world's largest man-made harbor.

CHEAPEST SECONDHAND FIRE ENGINES

The cheapest used fire engines in good operating condition are sold by the Los Angeles Fire Department for one dollar each.

Don't plan on buying one. You have to be either a needy municipality or a sister city. The fire wagons are distributed as a charitable program that supplies them on the basis of need. Two recipients: Mexico and Argentina.

BIGGEST TIRE PUNCTURER

Those snarling steel teeth that curl up at you at the exits of parking lots and threaten "WARNING! Severe Tire Damage" are known to the industry as Saber Teeth. The world's largest manufacturer of these tire-puncturing monsters is Delta Scientific of Burbank.

The company, which started in a garage in 1977, is now branching out into terrorist-stopping barricades and has more than 200 installed in U.S. embassies and offices around the world.

ONLY WOODEN LIGHTHOUSE

Many wooden lighthouses once protected sailors along California's inhospitable coast, but only one remains, a four-story tower on the edge of a cliff in Point Fermin Park, San Pedro.

The lighthouse was built in 1874 on a promontory that gave it the most commanding view of the ocean on the Southern California coast. It was used until 1942 and is now the official residence of the Point Fermin Park superintendent.

The first two lighthouse-keepers were sisters who quit because they couldn't stand the isolation, although the lighthouse had far more homey comforts than most.

FIRST LASER

The invention of the laser is clouded with conflicting claims and numerous lawsuits; nevertheless Los Angeles may lay legitimate claim to being its birthplace.

The first laser was built by a scientist named Naiman of the Hughes Research Institute in Malibu in 1960. His laser was based on a patent by physicists Charles Towner and Arthur Schwarow.

TOP AIRPORT APPROACH SPEED

Every jet plane must, as it reaches a point 50 miles from Los Angeles, slow down markedly. The speed limit for any aircraft flying in the Los Angeles International Airport TCA (Terminal Control Area) is 230 miles per hour.

The TCA stretches above the city in three dimensions. It is 24 miles wide and 52 miles long and is separated into 12 altitude layers.

LARGEST AIRPORT

In 1985 LAX was the number-one commercial airport in the L.A. area and third in the country. It registered 546,162 operations (a takeoff or a landing) and 350,070 of those were commercial air operations. Altogether 37,647,983 passengers flew either in or out of LAX.

SHORTEST RAILROAD

The shortest regularly scheduled passenger railroad in the Los Angeles area, indeed the shortest in the world in its time, was the Angels' Flight railway, which traveled three-fifths of a mile from the corner of 3rd and Hill streets to the top of Bunker Hill on a 33 percent grade.

The railroad, beloved by everyone but developers, carried more than 100 million passengers in its first 50 years and traveled more than 15.6 million miles from 1912 until its last run Sunday, May 18, 1969. Revenues in its last year were $250 a month against an operating coast of $2,000.

The equipment for the funicular railroad, including ticket office, station, cars, tracks, arches, etc., is in mothballs awaiting the fulfillment of a promise of the Community Redevelopment Agency (which dismantled it for a housing project) to restore the landmark railroad in a nearby location.

FIRST ROUND-THE-WORLD AIRCRAFT

The first aircraft to circumnavigate the globe were a pair of Douglas World Cruisers, designed and built in Santa Monica. They had an average air speed of 78 miles per hour.

MOST VICTORIAN HOMES

The biggest concentration of restored Victorian homes still in use is on the 300 block of Carroll Avenue. The block boasts ornate, magnificent gingerbread mansions from the glory years of the 1800s, when Angelino Heights was the most fashionable place to live.

FIRST MONORAIL

The first monorail was invented and built by a Los Angeles apricot farmer, Joseph Wesley Fawkes. In 1911 he built a cigar-shaped car, capable of carrying 56 passengers and driven by an airplane propeller and suspended from an iron rail. He named it the Aerial Swallow and made history's first and shortest monorail run, 150 feet.

Fawkes planned to make the run from Burbank to Los Angeles in ten minutes at 60 miles per hour. Unfortunately the Aerial Swallow fell apart on its first run. On its second, and probably last, run, it attained a top speed of three miles an hour.

Fawkes was the victim of quite a bit of mono-raillery. The locals dubbed the Aerial Swallow Fawkes' Folly. Nevertheless Fawkes had produced America's first patented monorail.

OLDEST CHURCH

The oldest place of worship in Los Angeles is Our Lady

Queen of Angels Church on North Main Street. It was built by Franciscan Fathers with the help of Indians in 1818–1822. Still standing, it has been declared a historic landmark.

BUSIEST INTERSECTION

No surface street intersection in Los Angeles handles as much traffic as the conjunction of Century and Aviation, which has a traffic flow of 120,267 cars daily. Second, Wilshire and Veteran, 115,243 cars daily.

BUSIEST STREET

The busiest surface street (as opposed to a freeway) in Los Angeles is Wilshire Boulevard, with a traffic count in Westwood of 106,000 vehicles a day. This is 26,000 more per day than the Glendale Freeway, which handles only 80,000 cars and trucks at its busiest point.

WORLD'S BUSIEST FREEWAY INTERSECTION

The point where the Ventura Freeway intersects the San Diego Freeway in Sherman Oaks is the busiest traffic junction in the world. Every 24 hours 458,000 vehicles fight their way through the intersection. Stopped totally, as they often are, the cars and trucks that pass through in 24 hours would form a solid rectangular parking lot from Los Angeles to Seattle, Washington.

BUSIEST FREEWAY

In 1986 the Ventura Freeway with a daily traffic flow of 267,000 vehicles supplanted the Santa Monica (240,000 vehicles per day) to become the nation's busiest freeway.

The San Diego Freeway has become the second busiest, with a daily traffic count of 266,000 at its busiest point, the juncture with Santa Monica Boulevard. Santa Monica Freeway is now third.

The previous world champion, the Dan Ryan Expressway in Chicago, boasts a mere trickle of 255,000 vehicles daily.

LARGEST DRY CLEANER

The largest over-the-counter dry cleaner in the United States is a one-hour service shop, Holloway Cleaners in West Hollywood, which dry cleans more than 8,000 garments and launders 8,000 to 10,000 pieces a week.

LARGEST REAL ESTATE TRANSACTION

The largest single real estate transaction in the history of Southern California was the sale of the Arco Plaza in downtown Los Angeles for $650 million.

The 52-story twin buildings were the tallest buildings in Southern California when they opened in 1972, and its classiest business address.

The building was jointly owned by Arco, hard hit by falling oil prices, and Bank of America, which suffered from bad management and enormous loan losses. B. of A. netted $200 million on the transaction, and ARCO an after-taxes profit of $80 million.

The skyscrapers were sold to an American subsidiary of Shuwa Co., a major commercial real estate firm in Japan.

MOST DANGEROUS INTERSECTION

The honor of being the most dangerous intersection in Los Angeles is shared by two intersections: Pico and Vermont, and Venice and Vermont, with 24 accidents each in 1984. The second most dangerous is Hollywood and Sunset, with 23 accidents.

FIRST OCEAN PIER

Stearns Wharf, still alive and well in Santa Barbara, Los Angeles's beach and bedroom playground, is the first ocean pier built in California. Construction was completed in 1872.

BEST TAP WATER

According to a Consumer's Union report, you can't even *buy* a better drink of water in the whole United States than Los Angelenos can get out of their kitchen faucet. Along with New York, Los Angeles has the best-tasting tap water in the United States.

Los Angeles water was given a rating of excellent, the highest possible, and better than Perrier, Canada Dry, or a dozen other bottled waters attained.

FASTEST-GROWING DEPRESSION CITY

During the Great Depression, a lot of people figured if they were going to be down and out, they'd rather be down and out in Beverly Hills. During the Depression Beverly Hills was the fastest-growing city in the United States.

FIRST OFF-SHORE OIL DRILLING

The ocean off Summerland, about six miles east of Santa Barbara, was the site in 1895 of the world's first off-shore oil drilling.

Twelve oil platforms off Santa Barbara Channel now produce 9,000 barrels daily—80 percent of all the oil currently taken from California federal waters. Today, Santa Barbara citizens probably lead the world in their loathing of oil platforms.

SHORTEST HOTEL ROOM RENTAL

Although certain motels offer special one-hour rates for "siestas," the shortest time for which an L.A. hotel room could ever be rented was one minute—at a rate of 25 cents a minute.

The per-minute rate was offered to between-planes travelers by Skytel when it first opened a sleeping facility at Los Angeles International Airport. The 25-cents-a-minute rate was found to be too confusing to the public and was dropped after two days in favor of an hourly fee.

MOST EXPENSIVE ACCOMMODATIONS

The most expensive rooms, inch for inch, hour for hour, you can rent in the Los Angeles area are offered by Skytel in the Tom Bradley International Airport. Offered to travelers in search of temporary rest, a 13½-by-6-foot single room rents for $15.00 for an hour's stay.

Only singles are offered, and you're not permitted to share your space with even a marriage certificate–carrying spouse. Since your spouse must take a separate room, that comes to $30 an hour, which projected for 24 hours would cost $720.00 a day.

With that comes air conditioning, twin bed, closet, ten-inch television set, overhead light, telephone, bathroom with shower and soap, Kleenex, toothbrush, and shampoo.

LARGEST MAN-MADE HARBOR

The largest man-made harbor for small craft in the world is Marina del Rey, born Bollona Creek. The creek emptied into the ocean through lowlands that were practically a bog until the City of Los Angeles, acting on an inspired and bold vision, decreed it should be dredged to form a marina.

LOWEST TAX RATE

The lowest tax rate of any of the 77 incorporated cities in Los Angeles County is enjoyed by the residents of Beverly Hills.

However, a house in Beverly Hills may be worth several times as much as the same house elsewhere, and since taxes are based on property values, the home owner will find himself paying higher taxes than people of neighboring communities.

BUSIEST SMALL-PLANE AIRPORT

The busiest small-plane airport in the Los Angeles area and perhaps in the world is the Van Nuys Airport, which handles no commercial airplane traffic but averages 492,382 operations (takeoffs and landings) per year.

MOST DANGEROUS AIRPORT

Of the airports serving the Los Angeles area, the most dangerous by far is the Los Angeles International Airport, LAX on your ticket.

After a certain hour at night pilots must throttle back engines and approach the runways from the ocean in order to comply with the noise abatement ordinances protecting the sleeping citizenry. The International Pilots Association has designated it as being in the most unsafe category.

LAX shares this dubious honor with airports in Hong Kong and a few other cities around the world at which pilots come in on a wing and a prayer.

LONGEST CONTINUING BUSINESS

The longest continuing business in the Los Angeles area, indeed in all of California, is Ducommun Inc., which was started in Los Angeles as a small watch-repair shop by a Swiss immigrant in 1849 and grew into a giant electronics conglomerate.

In 1986 it moved out of town a tiny piece down to Cypress. Ducommun Inc. is hugely successful, but go try to get a watch repaired.

FIRST FOUR-LEVEL FREEWAY INTERCHANGE

A wonder of the world when it was completed in 1949, and still a symbol of Los Angeles, is the four-level interchange of the Santa Ana, Harbor, Hollywood, and Pasadena freeways. The confluence of the sensuously curving roadways creates what some architects consider to be one of the world's most beautiful man-made structures.

It is one of the city's busiest interchanges, traveled by some 400,000 vehicles per day.

LARGEST ROSE GARDEN

Exposition Park, adjacent to the University of Southern California, is the world's largest rose garden, with 17,000 bushes of 150 varieties of roses. The peak bloom seasons are from April to May and September to October.

WORLD'S LARGEST CAMELLIA GARDENS

The world's largest collection of camellias, 100,000 gorgeous plants covering 165 acres, is to be found in La Canada at the county-maintained Descanso Gardens. Also, unique to Los Angeles County is Descanso's rose gardens featuring roses from ancient European monasteries.

LARGEST ATRIUM

Stretching 160 feet high and supported by a skeleton of tubes, the atrium at the Plaza Alicante in Garden Grove is the largest in the Los Angeles area and is said by its builder to be the largest in the western United States.

LARGEST GLASS BUILDING

The largest glass structure of any kind in the world is the Crystal Cathedral in Garden Grove.

LARGEST PHOTOGRAPH

The largest, most expensive photograph in the world was taken on July 7, 1984, of 16,000 Los Angelenos saying "cheese."

The photograph was taken to celebrate the Olympic Games. The city issued an open invitation to anyone who wanted to be in the world's largest photograph to show up at the 4th Street Overpass of the Harbor Freeway. Mayor Tom Bradley, Gregory Peck, and assorted singers and dancers joined the 16,000 ordinary hams. The finished picture cost $100,000 and is purported to be as large as three billboards. However, as of two years later, no one has seen it. Maybe it isn't back from the drugstore.

FINEST STAINED-GLASS WINDOW

Several Los Angeles art experts consider the mammoth stained-glass window in the chapel at Forest Lawn Cemetery in Glendale as the world's finest. It depicts Da Vinci's *Last Supper*.

FIRST MAN-POWERED AIRCRAFT

Paul MacCready, an aeronautical engineer from Pasadena, won the Kremer Prize for creating the world's first successful man-powered aircraft. His Gossamer Condor was flown by Bryan Allen over the required three-mile course on August 23, 1977. The craft had no engine except Bryan Allen pedaling away on a bicyclelike contraption.

FIRST TELEGRAPH

The first telegraph in the Western area, capable of reliably transmitting messages, was operated by the army at the Drum Barracks, located at what is now 1053 Cary Avenue in Los Angeles.

The barracks served as a base for operations against the Indians and as an officers' headquarters during the Civil War.

LARGEST DAILY PAPER

The largest daily paper in Los Angeles is the *Los Angeles Times*, which has an average daily circulation of 1,038,499, compared to its nearest rival, the *Herald-Examiner*, circulation 254,845. The *Los Angeles Times* exceeds the circulation of the *New York Times* by some 127,961 copies a day.

The *Los Angeles Times* prints enough pages daily to reach

from Los Angeles to Paris and back. In any list of the ten best newspapers of the nation, the L.A. *Times* is always included. It also appears on most lists of the 50 great papers of the world.

The L.A. *Times* is also the nation's largest standard-size daily newspaper.

OLDEST FREEWAY

The oldest freeway in the Los Angeles area is the Pasadena Freeway, which was dedicated on December 4, 1940, and opened on December 27, 1941. Originally named the Arroyo Seco Parkway, it begins at the downtown interchange and runs 8.5 miles to Pasadena.

CHEAPEST FREEWAY TO BUILD

The entire 8.5-mile Pasadena Freeway, which has three 12-foot-lanes in each direction and 18 bridges, was built at a total cost of $5 million, much less than the price of a single mile of freeway today.

OLDEST HOUSE

The oldest residence still standing in Los Angeles is the Avila Adobe, built in 1818 as a townhouse for Francisco Avila, a one-term mayor, when Los Angeles was still a pueblo.

The house is constructed of adobe brick with three-foot-thick walls and packed-earth floors. Door and window frames were imported from Boston.

It was damaged by earthquakes in 1870 and 1971, but has been restored as an example of the life-style of early Los Angeles and declared a State Historical Landmark. It is part of the El Pueblo de Los Angeles State Historical Park.

OLDEST WINERY

The oldest winery still in operation is the San Antonio winery at 737 Lamar Street, Los Angeles. Founded in 1917, it stores wine in wood casks, some of which are more than 100 years old. In 1966 the winery was declared a historic cultural monument.

ONLY MERRY-GO-ROUND APARTMENT

Often seen in movies, the apartment built above the merry-go-round on the Santa Monica Pier is the only merry-go-round apartment in the world. To paraphrase an old saying, "Run into the merry-go-round apartment, Nellie, he can't corner you there."

OLDEST HELICOPTERS

The L.A. Fire Department flies several Bell 206 B. Jetrangers said to be the oldest fleet of Jetrangers in the world, one-third of them averaging more than 20,000 hours.

The Fire Department also flies Bell 47's, the chopper used in the series "M*A*S*H." Top speed is 150 miles per hour, but they usually cruise at 70 miles per hour, about 600 feet above the city.

In a typical year Fire Department helicopters will douse fires with more than a million gallons of water and rescue some 1,000 people.

MOST EXPENSIVE STREET DECORATIONS

No city in the Los Angeles area, possibly in the world, has ever spent more on street decorations than did Beverly Hills in 1986 when, in order to compete with the malls for

Christmas shoppers, the city fathers strung baubles and lights above its streets to the tune of $2 million.

Beautiful downtown Burbank spends about $2,500.

LARGEST MANSION EVER BUILT

The largest mansion ever built in the Los Angeles area was built in 1925 by William Randolph Hearst in Santa Monica for girlfriend Marion Davies. Built on the beach and named Ocean House, it contained 118 rooms, 37 fireplaces, and 55 bathrooms. As he did when he built San Simeon, Hearst imported many 16th-century rooms from Europe and had them installed in Ocean House. The building at 415 Palisades Beach Road was destroyed by fire, but the servants' quarters and a guest house remain and are used as a private club.

HIGHEST PRICE FOR A SINGLE-FAMILY HOME

In 1981 singer Kenny Rogers purchased a Bel Air home from producer Dino DeLaurentiis for $14.5 million which, at the time, was not only a Los Angeles record, but also a national record for a single-family home.

Only a few years before Rogers had trouble scraping together $300 to pay his monthly rent on an apartment.

The 35-room house, which was built in 1955, features such luxuries as a black-and-white marble center hallway, white marble fireplace in the living room, and silk-lined cabinets in the dining room, plus a four-passenger elevator. The two master bedrooms have a sitting room that opens onto an upstairs veranda spanning the width of the house.

Other goodies: a film-screening room, 48-foot pool, a pool house with covered terrace, and a 13-car garage complete with a fully equipped mechanic's shop, hydraulic lift, and underground gas tank and pump. Eight hundred thousand dollars' worth of furniture came with the house.

In 1984 Rogers sold the house to Marvin Davis, then owner of 20th Century-Fox, for a price which set a new record, $22.5 million.

MOST HOMELESS

The greatest number of people without a place to live and officially designated as homeless was reached in Los Angeles in 1986, when it was estimated that 33,000 people, including complete families, were living in the streets. The luckier ones found cardboard boxes in which to set up housekeeping.

OLDEST RESTAURANT IN LOS ANGELES

Founded in 1908, the oldest continuously operating restaurant in the city of Los Angeles and declared a historical monument is the Coles P. E. Buffet, at 118 E. 6th Street.

OLDEST RESTAURANT IN HOLLYWOOD

The oldest restaurant in Hollywood is Musso and Franks, 6667 Hollywood Boulevard, founded in 1919.

LARGEST COFFEE-SHOP CHAIN

The world's largest coffee-shop chain is Los Angeles–based Denny's, with 123 restaurants in the Los Angeles area and 12,000 nationally.

LARGEST FOLK ART SCULPTURE

The largest piece of folk art ever created by a single person is the Simon Rhodia Towers, 1765 E. 107th Street in Watts.

Simon Rhodia, a tile setter, labored 33 years on his masterpiece, beginning it in 1921 and ending it in 1954. He lived in a house on the property.

This work consists of three towers, the highest in the center being 104 feet, surrounded by a wall. Not only is it an artistic triumph, the engineering itself astounds experts. In 1959 bureaucrats wanted to knock it down because they deemed it a hazard, likely to fall on someone. They tried to demolish it with a hydraulic jack, exerting pressure of 10,000 pounds on the main tower. During the attempt the jack itself broke.

The towers, their worth finally realized, are now protected by the city, state, and federal governments.

They contain thousands of bits of china and glass, and 7,000 sea shells collected by Rhodia over the years. Rumor has it that morsels of his old Hudson car are embedded in the towers and its skeleton is buried nearby.

Once he finished the towers, the then 75-year-old Rhodia deeded the lot and his work to a neighbor and disappeared.

OLDEST MUSEUM

The oldest museum in Los Angeles is the Southwest Museum in Highland Park, founded in 1907.

It houses more than a half-million artifacts of native American Mexicans and Indians and of the early settlers, side by side with the works of contemporary Indian artists.

NEWEST MUSEUM

The newest museum in Los Angeles is the Museum of Contemporary Art, which opened downtown in 1986.

RICHEST MUSEUM

The J. Paul Getty Museum in Malibu is L.A.'s and the world's richest. It *must*, under the terms of its tax-free status, spend its income, estimated to be more than a million dollars a day, on art purchases. The museum must exercise conscious restraint on how much it will bid for works of art, or it could literally corner the world's art treasures.

MOST PHOTOGRAPHED MUSEUM

The Norton Simon Museum in Pasadena (the exterior) has been seen by more people than any other museum in the world. The museum is across the street from the television cameras that photograph the Rose Parade. The museum is seen in the background of at least half the shots and thus is familiar to millions of people in the United States and around the world.

LARGEST NATURAL HISTORY MUSEUM

The Natural History Museum at 900 Exposition Boulevard is the largest in the Los Angeles area and the largest west of the Mississippi.

Opened in 1913, it contains 8½ acres of floor space. It is noted for exhibits of gems and minerals, animal life, pre-Columbian artifacts, and southwestern history. Two dinosaurs and a mummy greet visitors in the foyer.

LARGEST FIND OF PLEISTOCENE REMAINS

The La Brea Tar Pits on Wilshire Boulevard contain bubbling pools of asphaltum and crude oil which thousands of centuries ago in the Ice Age trapped mammoths, giant sloths, saber-tooth tigers, and other prehistoric monsters in its implacable tarlike ooze. The trapped animals have so far yielded more than 600,000 prehistoric bones, the world's largest find of Pleistocene remains.

The La Brea Tar Pits are still bubbling and are open to the public in the George C. Page Museum at the Rancho La Brea Tar Pits, which is a satellite of the Natural History Museum.

MOST IMPORTANT ART ACQUISITION

The most important acquisition in Los Angeles and one of the most important in the United States in the last 50 years is an ancient Greek marble sculpture, *Kouras*, acquired by the J. Paul Getty Art Museum in 1985. The statue is a nude, 6 foot 7 inches, of a young man. *Kouras* means young man. The authenticity of the statue was contested by Italian experts and was purchased by the Getty Museum only after several years of meticulous examination by scholars. The statue, which is in an extraordinary state of preservation, stands upright without visible support, and may be the world's first to be "earthquake-proofed." The musuem's conservator of antiquities, Jerry Podany, connected severed parts of the body with flexible ¼-inch steel cables, instead of the usual steel rods, and floats the statue upon a centered ball bearing.

LARGEST ART MUSEUM

If all proceeds as planned, the largest museum complex in

the area will be the proposed J. Paul Getty Fine Arts Center in the Santa Monica Mountains above Brentwood. The whole complex, which includes a 250,000-square-foot museum to house the art treasures now in the Malibu Museum, will feature an art history and humanities research facility with a world-class library, a conservation institute, an auditorium for lectures, restaurants, and 30 apartments to house visiting scholars.

The center will occupy 24 acres of a 105-acre site. The museum complex will total 450,000 square feet. By comparison the County Museum of Art is 246,000 square feet and the Museum of Contemporary Art 100,000 square feet.

LARGEST GIFT TO A UNIVERSITY

The largest gift of any kind ever made to any university anywhere, by anyone, is the gift from Norton Simon, 80, of his art collection to UCLA. The art collection is considered by connoisseurs to be the finest compendium of Old Masters, classic, modern, and rare Asian art assembled by any single individual in the last half-century.

With the acquisition of these art treasures, UCLA will have the greatest University-based art collection in the world.

MOST VALUABLE STAMP

The most valuable stamp ever owned by anyone in Los Angeles is an 1876 "1-cent Z grill" U.S. stamp, of which only two exist in the world. It was bought by millionaire sportsman Jerry Buss (owner of the Forum, the Kings, the Lakers) who purchased the stamp at auction in 1977 for $100,000.

Four years later he refused $330,000 for it. Shortly after,

he felt he was too busy to take care of his collection and commissioned the Superior Stamp Company to sell his "1-cent Z grill." At an auction at the Century City Hotel in November 1986, it was sold for $383,000. It was the second most expensive stamp ever sold in philatelic history.

MOST EXPENSIVE DOLL

The most expensive doll ever purchased in Los Angeles, or for that matter anywhere in the world, is a 19th-century French doll known as Long Faced Jumeau, which was purchased by an unknown buyer at a Los Angeles auction for $45,000.

The doll is of an adult woman made in the 1880s by Emilke Jumeau Co. of Paris. It is a 29-inch blue-eyed *jumeau tristes*, with a bisque head and a pressed wood pulp body. She is dressed in a royal blue gown trimmed with bronze silk and ecru lace. She is crowned with a mohair wig, wears a tan straw hat, pearl earrings, and black leather shoes. Old Sad Eyes was sold by Theriaults, the Doll Masters, a national auction house.

LARGEST GLASS SCULPTURE

The largest single piece of carved glass in the world is that created by sculptor Suzanne Pascal in her Beverly Hills backyard studio. The massive, ice green seated figure is carved from a nine-foot-tall slab of glass rescued from an abandoned factory, and weighs nine tons.

Few diamonds in the world are as valuable; the raw glass is insured for $3 million. Completed in 1987, the nine-foot monolith had to be studied like a diamond for flaws and stress lines, and cut to reveal its liquid light. The process took ten years.

UNIVERSITY TEACHING MOST FOREIGN LANGUAGES

No institution in the world teaches as many foreign languages as the nearly 100 taught at UCLA.

LARGEST LIBRARY

The main branch of the Los Angeles Public Library system, known as the Central Branch, was, until a disastrous arson fire in 1986, the largest library in the West. It houses more than two million items valued at more than $60 million. The library is being energetically restored.

MYSTERY BOOKS

The largest stock of mystery books in the Los Angeles area is the 25,000- to 50,000-selection at Sherman Oaks Scene of the Crime bookstore, which sells only detective stories and answers to the cutesy telephone number, 981-CLUE.

LARGEST COLLECTION OF JEWISH BOOKS

The largest selection of Jewish books in the United States is offered by J. Roth, Bookseller, at 9427 West Pico. The store stocks 10,000 different titles, including religious school texts.

LARGEST COMIC BOOK COLLECTION

The world's largest collection of comic books is owned by the American Comic Book Company, 12206 Ventura Boulevard in Studio City, which specializes in back issues and rare editions. Their collection boasts more than one million comic books and more than 100,000 first-edition science-fiction magazines.

LARGEST CONCENTRATION OF TV ANTENNAS

Clustered on top of the 5,713-foot summit of Los Angeles's Mt. Wilson, known as Television Peak, is the largest concentration of television, radio, and communication transmitters in the United States.

Over 75,000 tourists a year visit the towers located on each side of Skyline Drive at the aptly named intersection of Audio and Video roads.

LARGEST COLLECTION OF MECHANICAL MUSICAL INSTRUMENTS

The world's largest collection of mechanical musical instruments is the Merle Norman Classic Beauty Collection in Sylmer. The museum features more than 200 windup violins, automatic banjoes, nickelodeons, and giant orchestrians in jukeboxlike cases with horns, accordians, violins, and piano all playing together.

MOST BOOKS FOR SALE

The largest seller of new books, both hardcover and paperbacks, on the West Coast is B. Dalton, originally the Pickwick Bookstore, located at 6743 Hollywood Boulevard. The store stocks between 25,000 and 35,000 titles.

FIRST UNIVERSITY

The first university in the Los Angeles area was the

University of Southern California, founded in 1879 by Methodists.

MOST SISTER CITIES

Under the aegis of Sister Cities International, cities from all parts of the world adopt each other as sisters for the purpose of making "significant friendly cultural exchanges." Lately a vulture for culture, no city has more sisters than Los Angeles, which is Sister City to 14: Athens, Greece; Auckland, New Zealand; Bombay, India; Bordeaux, France; Eilat, Israel; Guangzhou, China; Nagoya, Japan; Pusan, Korea; Lusaka, Zambia; Mexico City, Mexico; Salvador, Brazil; Taipei, Taiwan; Teheran, Iran; and West Berlin, West Germany.

As in any large family, sibling quarrels occur, and currently Los Angeles and sister Teheran are not speaking; their affiliation has been suspended. Perhaps if L.A. were to sell them arms . . . ?

OLDEST HOME IN HOLLYWOOD

The oldest home in Hollywood is an adobe structure located in the Farmer's Market and was the birthplace of Earl Gilmore, the market's founder. The home was built in 1852 and it was Gilmore's home until his death in 1964. His bedroom is kept exactly as it was at the time of his death more than 20 years ago.

LARGEST EGG RANCH

The largest egg ranch in the world is Ventura County's Egg City, where three million hens lay more than two million eggs a day.

LARGEST TOY FACTORY

The largest toy manufacturer in the world is Mattel, Inc. of Hawthorne, founded in 1945 at the start of the postwar baby boom.

LARGEST HOLOCAUST MUSEUM

Scheduled to open in 1988, the Simon Wiesenthal Center complex in West Los Angeles will be the largest exhibit in the world devoted to documenting intolerance. Centerpiece of the $24-million, 78,000-square-foot complex will be the Beit HaShoah "House of the Holocaust."

FANCIEST MCDONALD'S

L.A.'s and perhaps the world's fanciest McDonald's is located on the Plaza Level of the Crocker Center, whose twin towers are home to some of the city's most upscale corporations and law firms.

The restaurant, a symphony of polished brass, Grecian marble, brick floors, and gleaming wood tables, features fresh flowers on the tables, free newspapers, plug-in phones (which can be rushed to your booth if you want to make a call), and a harpist who plays every Thursday and Friday.

CHEAPEST PARKING METERS

The cheapest parking meters in Los Angeles are those on York Boulevard, where the rate is ten cents an hour. Los Angeles, with 31,000 parking meters, claims they are the cheapest of any major city in the United States, and as of 1986 is planning on doubling the rates.

ONLY HIGH SCHOOL WITH ITS OWN OIL WELLS

The only high school in the Los Angeles area and perhaps in the world that has operating oil rigs in the schoolyard is Beverly Hills High School, with two rigs that generate $1,800 to $2,500 a month in royalties. During the oil glut when oil prices plunged, Beverly Hills, like many nations, had to consider raising taxes to make up for lost revenue.

LARGEST BUILDING SHAPED LIKE A PRODUCT

The world's largest building shaped to advertise its business and the world's first circular office building is the 14-story Capital Records edifice just north of Hollywood and Vine, shaped to look like a stack of 45-r.p.m. records, complete with a giant stylus on top.

MOST EXPENSIVE RESIDENTIAL REAL ESTATE

The most expensive real estate in metropolitan Los Angeles is the area lying north of Sunset in Beverly Hills in the 800, 900, and 1000 blocks. Next most expensive, in order, are Old Bel Air, Malibu, Riviera section of the Pacific Palisades, Santa Monica.

LARGEST SHOPPING CENTER

The largest shopping center in the United States with 2.9 million square feet is the South Coast Plaza. The Del Amo Fashion Center in Torrence is second.

LARGEST POST OFFICE

The largest post office in the Los Angeles area is the Main Post Office, located downtown at 300 North Los

Angeles Street. Handling 3,752 million pieces of mail a year, Los Angeles's postal service ranks second in size only to that of New York.

LARGEST SPORTSWEAR INDUSTRY

The downtown garment district in southeast Los Angeles is the world's largest manufacturing center for sportswear and casual clothes.

LARGEST LAUNDRY

The largest laundry in Los Angeles, indeed the largest laundry outside New York City, is that of the Los Angeles County–U.S.C. Medical Center, which washes twenty tons of sheets and scrub suits a day.

LARGEST SWAP MEET

With 1,500 dealers selling merchandise from tailgates, the Rose Bowl Swap Meet is the L.A. area's largest. The merchants gather in an enormous ring which circles the Bowl on the second Sunday of every month.

Tied for second: Saugus Swap Meet and Costa Mesa, both with 1,200 dealers, every Sunday.

LARGEST MEMORIAL PARK

Rose Hills Memorial Park, which stretches across 2,600 acres in Whittier, is the world's largest memorial park, named for the 750 varieties of roses and 7,000 rose bushes that adorn the park.

LARGEST MUNICIPAL PARK

The largest municipal park in the United States is Griffith Park, which covers 4,000 acres. Originally called Los Feliz Ranch, it was donated to Los Angeles by Colonel J. Griffith in 1896.

MOST EXPENSIVE CHRISTMAS TREE DECORATIONS

The value of the ornaments on the Cartier Christmas tree exhibited in Beverly Hills in 1984 was $9 million. The tree honored with this munificence was an artificial pine. In the true spirit of Christmas, the tree was protected by three armed guards not even dressed as elves.

MOST EXPENSIVE ARTIFICIAL CHRISTMAS TREE

The most expensive artificial Christmas tree ever purchased was bought in 1985 by the South Coast Plaza, a shopping center, for $40,000.

WORST INSULT TO BING CROSBY'S TASTE

In 1983 television producer Aaron Spelling bought the Bing Crosby mansion in Holmby Hills for $10.5 million. As soon as the house was safely his, he tore it down.

MOST EXPENSIVE MCDONALD'S

The most expensive to build McDonald's is the one at 6776 Hollywood Boulevard, which opened in 1987 at a cost of $3 million.

The restaurant features the glitziest, gaudiest set of golden arches of the whole 7,000-restaurant chain, thus helping to preserve, the builders believe, the show biz tradition of Hollywood.

WEALTHIEST ZIP CODE

The wealthiest ZIP code in the United States is believed to be ZIP code 90210. It embraces all of Rodeo Drive, all of Beverly Hills north of Wilshire (the famous "flats"), and part of Benedict Canyon. Average after-tax income is claimed to be $122,000 per family.

HIGHEST PRICE PAID BY A CANDIDATE FOR VOTES

The most money ever spent by any candidate to win public office in California is $102 per vote. Gene La Pietra, a millionaire nightclub owner, spent this sum in pursuit of a seat on the West Hollywood City Council. He lost! His opponent, who won, Abbe Land, spent $6.22 per vote.

La Pietra's campaign was hurt by disclosures that he had made some of his money in pornographic films and books and had been convicted on federal and state criminal obscenity charges.

The most costly assembly race in California history was that of Tom Hayden (D. Santa Monica), husband of Jane Fonda. He spent $1.3 million or $20.02 per vote to win in 1982.

Sports and Personal Achievements

LOS ANGELES, creator of spectaculars, host of the Olympics, worshiper of fitness, is a premier generator of great athletes and record-breaking gates. To be the best in Los Angeles is often to be the best in the world.

But it is not the nature of Los Angeles to confine its prowess to the conventional sports; frivolous challenges beckon. Can you eat more doughnuts in three minutes? Have you collected more string, married more women, had more face-lifts? Can you stand on one foot or spin in a laundry dryer longer than anyone in Los Angeles?

Immortality is where you find it. If you're the best in L.A., let us hear from you. If we can authenticate your claim, you belong in this book.

FASTEST CARD THROWER

No man has ever thrown a playing card with the speed, accuracy, and height achieved by magician and author (*Learned Pigs & Fireproof Women*) Ricky Jay, who can throw a card faster than most major league pitchers can throw a ball. His cards have been timed at 90 miles an hour.

He can slice ash off a cigarette held in a man's mouth with a thrown playing card and has achieved what is believed to be a world's record by throwing a standard playing card over a two-story house.

ONLY BEVERLY HILLS HIGH GRAD TO BECOME A MATADOR

Graduates of Beverly Hills High School have gone on to do their share of running the world, but only one has become a matador and fought in a bull ring. That one graduate is Phil Ritz of the famous Ritz Brothers.

LONGEST MOVIE KISS

Kissing is both a sport and an achievement. No records of civilian kisses in Los Angeles exist at the moment, but historians tell us the longest kiss in films was in the movie *You're in the Army Now* and lasted 3 minutes and 15 seconds.

MOST BALLOONS RELEASED

The most balloons ever released at one time is one million—sent aloft by Disneyland in celebration of what would have been Walt Disney's 84th birthday. This world's record has since been broken in Cleveland.

CONDOM-THROWING COMPETITION

The world's first distance competition for throwing water-filled condoms was held in 1986 at USC by a nonprofit organization called Pharmacy Planning Service, which is trying to increase condom awareness as suggested by the United States Surgeon General. The condom throwing was part of a decathlon of condom-connected events including a blow-up contest. Official records are not available for this first event, but future records will be.

LONGEST WALK ON HOT COALS

The longest walk in bare feet over hot coals without hypnotism or any protective preparation was achieved on the beach at Santa Monica on New Year's Eve, 1985, by Linda Lief, who walked 35 feet over 2,000-degree coals.

Ms. Lief was part of a class in neuro-linguistics taught by the Robbins Research Institute, and the fire walk was a sort of graduation ceremony to prove that nothing is impossible. About 50 ordinary people did some fire-walking that New Year's Eve.

MOST WOMEN'S ARM-WRESTLING CHAMPIONSHIPS

The top woman arm wrestler in the Los Angeles area is Lori Cole of Encino, who since 1980 has won six world championships. Her technique is to "flash" an opponent: forcing the arm down in a burst of irresistible force in the first second or two. She finds protracted matches strenuous; in one Lori's spirit was unyielding, but her arm broke.

FIRST SURFER

The first surfer to dip board into foam in the United States was George Freeth of Hawaii, who introduced the sport at Redondo Beach in 1907. He was brought here by the Pacific Electric Railroad, which promoted surfing in order to bolster trolley traffic to Redondo.

FASTEST WATER-SKIER

The fastest water-skier in the Los Angeles area and eventually the fastest in the world was Chuck Stearns of Bellflower, who on December 17, 1966, skied into the record books at Marine Studium, Long Beach, with a world speed record of 119.52 miles per hour.

SMALLEST AIRPLANE

The smallest plane built in Los Angeles or indeed anywhere in the world is that constructed by Donald Stits, 36, of Newbury Park. His airplane, Baby Bird, was built in his garage weekends over a five-year period at a cost of about $5,000. It weights 452 pounds empty and is just under 10 feet long. It has a wing spread of 7 feet 2 inches and an air speed of about 182 miles per hour.

LONGEST BURRITO

The longest burrito in the Los Angeles area and perhaps in the world was concocted at Juniper Park in Fontana by the Fontana Youth Association, which sold slices as a fund-raising effort. The burrito, spread out over 33 tables, was confected of 312 tortillas filled with 50 pounds of frijoles.

The chefs would have made the burrito even bigger, but

they ran out of tables and space when it reached a record-breaking 312 feet.

FIRST FLIGHT-ENDURANCE RECORD

In the skies over Los Angeles, between January 1 and 7, 1929, Air Corps Major Carl Spaatz and Captain Ira Eaker established the first flight-endurance record in history by remaining aloft in their Army Fokker for 150 hours and 40 minutes.

FIRST CROSS-COUNTRY FLIGHT BY BLACKS

In 1932, an era when it was the policy of the Army Air Corps not to admit blacks and when commercial aviation likewise denied them jobs, two black Los Angelenos, Herman Banning and Thomas Allen, completed a historic flight from Los Angeles to Long Island, New York, the first cross-country flight by blacks.

Their plane was a flying bundle of bolts, a heavenly hash of bits and pieces scavenged from wrecked or ancient aircraft found in plane graveyards. The 3,300-mile trip took 42 hours in the air, spread over 21 days since the team had to stop along the way to raise money to continue. Among their tasks, dropping campaign leaflets in three cities for Franklin D. Roosevelt.

In those days Los Angeles was the nation's capital for black flyers who met professional rejection elsewhere.

GLIDER ALTITUDE RECORD

No man has flown higher in a glider than Bob Harris, a hardware store owner of Riverside who, on February 17, 1986, set the world altitude record of 49,009 feet.

With jaunty California nonchalance he neglected both to wear a pressurized suit and get permission from the FAA for his flight through jet plane lanes. He survived the life-threatening cold and the nonpressurized cabin, but the FAA was more formidable. He is still fighting a loss of license and a fine. However, his record has been certified and stands..

FIRST SUPERSONIC FLIGHT

The first supersonic flight in California or anywhere for that matter took place at Muroc Air Force Base on October 14, 1947, when Chuck Yeager flew a U.S. Bell XS Rocket plane at Mach 1.015, 670 miles per hour.

FIRST CHINESE GYMNAST

The first Chinest gymnast to represent an American university is Li Xiao Ping of Cal State Fullerton. Li was a member of the People's Republic of China team, which won the silver medal in the 1984 Olympics, and has received a perfect 10 on the pommel horse five times.

LARGEST HORSE-RACING HANDLE

The handle of the nine-race Breeders' Cup at Santa Anita Race Track, November 1, 1986, broke the record of $13.1 million set at the Kentucky Derby to become the largest take in the history of North American horse racing, $15,410,409.

FASTEST CAR DRIVER

In 1979 a Hollywood race car driver, Stan Barrett, was

the fastest man in the world. At Bonneville Flats in Utah he drove a 48,000-horsepower rocket car to a world record of 638.637 miles per hour.

FIRST DRIVER TO BREAK 600 MILES PER HOUR

Angeleno Craig Breedlove, in 1965, became the first man in history to travel more than 600 miles an hour on land when, in his Spirit of America–Sonic I, he attained an average speed of 613.995 miles per hour.

The car weighed 9,000 pounds and was 34 feet, 7 inches long. It was powered with a General Electric J 79 GE 3 Turbo-jet engine with an afterburner and could develop 15,000 pounds of thrust.

LARGEST RACETRACK WIN

The most money ever won by a single bettor at a racetrack was $1.9 million at Santa Anita in 1985 by Craig Phillips of Hacienda Heights who hit the Pick Nine.

LARGEST STADIUM

The largest stadium in Los Angeles and one of the largest in the world is the Rose Bowl, completed in 1922, with a seating capacity of 57,000. After many additions, the stadium now boasts a capacity of 104,091.

LARGEST CROWD

The largest crowd ever to view a sports event in Los Angeles history jammed into the Rose Bowl for the 1973 game between USC and Ohio State. Somehow exceeding its capacity by some 2,000, the Bowl was host to 106,869 fans.

RECORD-BREAKING HEPTATHLETE

Jackie Joyner-Kersee of UCLA became the first heptathlete to break the 7,000-point barrier with 7,148 points at the Goodwill Games in July 1986. Joyner-Kersee broke that record less than a month later by scoring 7,158 points at the U.S. Olympic Festival.

LARGEST SPORTS PURCHASE IN HISTORY

The largest transaction in the history of sports took place in 1979 when Jerry Buss, a Ph.D. in chemistry, purchased the L.A. Lakers, Kings, and the Forum from Jack Kent Cooke for $67.5 million. Buss and his family also own the L.A. Lazers of the Major Indoor Soccer League and the L.A. Strings pro-team tennis group. They recently founded L.A.'s first cable sports network, Prime Ticket, which broadcasts Forum–based teams and events, along with other pro and college games.

LARGEST LIVE BOXING GATE

The largest audience for a live boxing match and the largest take ($475,640) in West Coast history was paid by the audience at the Forum on September 10, 1973, to see Muhammad Ali and Ken Norton fight to a split decision.

PROFESSIONAL BASEBALL RECORDS

Los Angeles became a major league baseball city in 1958 when the Brooklyn Dodgers deserted the Big Apple for the Big Orange. In 1961 L.A. gave birth to one of the two first expansion teams in the majors with the formation of the American League's Los Angeles Angels.

The next year the Dodgers moved from the Coliseum, the largest stadium in the area, to their new cozy 56,000-seat home in Chavez Ravine.

The Los Angeles Angels moved to their permanent home, the 64,573-seat Anaheim Stadium, and changed their name to the California Angels.

An intense rivalry exists. However, in all-time records, the Dodgers seem to have the edge.

Largest Baseball Crowd

The crowd that gathered at the Coliseum on May 7, 1959, for an exhibition game between the Los Angeles Dodgers and the New York Yankees to honor Roy Campanella was the largest ever to assemble for any baseball event. The game drew a record-breaking 93,103 paid admissions.

Biggest Crowd for a Regular-Season Game

The largest crowd ever to witness a baseball game played in the regular season was 78,672 at the Los Angeles Coliseum in a game between the L.A. Dodgers and the San Francisco Giants, April 18, 1958.

Largest World Series Crowd

The record for paid attendance at a World Series game was set at the Los Angeles Coliseum, October 6, 1959, in a game between the L.A. Dodgers and the Chicago White Sox, which drew 92,706 fans.

Individual Hitting

The best batting records in one game are:
MOST HITS: 6, by Willie Davis (Dodgers) in a 19-inning game May 24, 1973.

MOST. R.B.I.s: 8, batted in first by Lee Thomas (Angels) against the K.C. Athletics in L.A., September 5, 1961.

This record was tied by:

Leon Wagner (Angels) vs. the Washington Senators in L.A. September 28, 1961.

Don Baylor (Angels) vs. the Blue Jays at Toronto August 25, 1979.

Ron Cey (Dodgers) vs. the San Diego Padres in L.A. July 31, 1974.

MOST HOME RUNS: 3, accomplished twice by Doug DeCinces against the Minnesota Twins in Anaheim August 2, 1982, and August 8, 1982, vs. Seattle Mariners at the Kingdome.

Seven other players have equaled this record in one game:

Don Demeter (Dodgers) vs. S.F. Giants in 11 innings April 21, 1959.

Jim Wynn (Dodgers) vs. San Diego Padres May 11, 1974.

Davey Lopes (Dodgers) vs. Chicago Cubs August 20, 1974.

Lee Thomas (Angels) vs. K.C. Athletics September 5, 1961.

Lee Stanton (Angels) vs. Pittsburgh Pirates July 10, 1973.

Carney Lansford (Angels) vs. Cleveland Indians September 1, 1979.

Fred Patek (Angels) vs. Boston Red Sox June 20, 1980.

Batting Records for a Single Season

LONGEST HITTING STREAK: 31 games, by Willie Davis (Dodgers) from August 1 to September 3, 1969. Not only was it the longest in L.A. history, but the fourth longest in modern National League history.

MOST CONSECUTIVE STOLEN BASES: 38 straight bases without being thrown out were stolen by Davey Lopes (Dodgers) in 1975 from June 10 through August 24 to set not only a Los Angeles but a major league record as well.

HIGHEST BATTING AVERAGE .346, Tommy Davis (Dodgers) in 1962.

MOST R.B.I.s: 153, Tommy Davis (Dodgers) in 1962.

MOST TOTAL HITS: 230, Tommy Davis (Dodgers) in 1962.

MOST TOTAL BASES: 356, Tommy Davis (Dodgers) in 1962.

HIGHEST SLUGGING PERCENTAGE: .615, Reggie Smith (Dodgers) in 1977.

MOST SINGLES: 179, Maury Wills (Dodgers) in 1962.

MOST DOUBLES: 47, Wes Parker (Dodgers) in 1970.

MOST TRIPLES: 16, Willie Davis (Dodgers) in 1970.

MOST HOME RUNS: 39, Reggie Jackson (Angels) in 1982.

MOST GRAND-SLAM HOMERS: 3, Joe Rudi (Angels) did it twice, in 1978 and in 1979.

MOST AT BATS: 695, Maury Wills (Dodgers) in 1962.

MOST STOLEN BASES: 104, Maury Wills (Dodgers) in 1962.

MOST PINCH HITS: 16, Winston Llenas (Angels) in 1973.

MOST BASES ON BALLS: 110, Jim Wynn (Dodgers) in 1975.

MOST SACRIFICE HITS: 26, Tim Foli (Angels) in 1982.

MOST SACRIFICE FLIES: 13, Reggie Smith (Dodgers) in 1978; tied by Dan Ford (Angels) in 1979.

MOST STRIKEOUTS: 156, Reggie Jackson (Angels) in 1982.

MOST HIT BY A PITCH: 18, a record tied by two sore Angels—Rich Reichardt in 1968 and Don Baylor in 1978.

MOST GAMES PLAYED: 165, Maury Wills's (Dodgers) feat is a major league record.

MOST GROUNDED INTO DOUBLE PLAYS: 26, Lyman Bostock (Angels) in 1978.

Team Batting Records

The top hitting in a single game by a team are:

MOST HITS: 26, Angels against Blue Jays in Toronto August 25, 1979 and again vs. Boston Red Sox in Boston June 20, 1980.

MOST RUNS SCORED, GAME: 24, Angels vs. Blue Jays in Toronto August 25, 1979.

MOST RUNS SCORED, INNING: 13, Angels, in 9th inning in Texas against Rangers September 14, 1978.

MOST HOME RUNS: 7, Dodgers accomplished this twice May 5, 1976, vs. Chicago Cubs at Wrigley Field and May 25, 1979, vs. Cincinnati Reds.

MOST TOTAL BASES: 52, Angels against Boston Red Sox at Fenway Park June 20, 1980.

MOST STOLEN BASES: 8, Dodgers vs. St. Louis Cardinals August 24, 1974.

MOST ERRORS: 7, Dodgers vs. Cincinnati Reds September 4, 1972.

Individual Pitching Records, Season

MOST WINS: 27, Sandy Koufax (Dodgers) 1966, is also a National League record.

MOST STRIKEOUTS: 383, Nolan Ryan (Angels) 1973, breaking Sandy Koufax's (Dodgers) record of 382 set in 1965, which still is a major league record for left-handed pitchers.

MOST GAMES: 106, Mike Marshall (Dodgers) 1974, is also a major league record.

MOST GAMES FINISHED: 83, Mike Marshall (Dodgers) 1974, also a major league record.

LOWEST EARNED-RUN AVERAGE: 1.36, Ken Tatum (Angels) 1969.
HIGHEST WINNING PCT.: .933 (14–1), Phil Regan (Dodgers) 1966.
MOST SHUTOUTS: 11, Sandy Koufax (Dodgers) 1963 and tied by Dean Chance (Angels) 1964.
MOST COMPLETE GAMES: 27, Sandy Koufax (Dodgers) 1965 and again 1966.
MOST SAVES: 31, Donnie Moore (Angels) 1985.
MOST GAMES STARTED: 42, Don Drysdale (Dodgers) 1963 and again 1965.
MOST INNINGS PITCHED: 336, Sandy Koufax (Dodgers) 1965.
MOST GAMES LOST: 19, George Brunet (Angels) 1967 tied by Clyde Wright (Angels) 1973 and Frank Tanana (Angels) 1974.
MOST RUNS: 127, Don Sutton (Dodgers) 1970 and tied by Nolan Ryan (Angels) 1974.
MOST EARNED RUNS: 118, Don Sutton (Dodgers) 1970.
MOST HITS: 298, Claude Osteen (Dodgers) 1967.
MOST HOME RUNS: 38, Don Sutton (Dodgers) 1970.
MOST BASES ON BALLS: 204, Nolan Ryan (Angels) 1977.
MOST HIT BATSMEN: 21, Tom Murphy (Angels) 1969.
MOST WILD PITCHES: 21, Nolan Ryan (Angels) 1977.
MOST NO-HITTERS (CAREER): , Sandy Koufax (Dodgers) vs. Chicago Cubs September 9, 1965—a perfect game. vs. New York Mets June 30, 1962. vs. San Francisco Giants May 11, 1963. vs. Philadelphia Phillies June 4, 1964. 4, Nolan Ryan (Angels) vs. Kansas City Royals May 15, 1973. vs. Detroit Tigers July 15, 1973. vs. Minnesota Twins September 28, 1974. vs. Baltimore Orioles June 1, 1975.

LONGEST WINNING STREAK FOR STARTING PITCHER: 12 games, Burt Hooten (Dodgers) from July 24, 1974, until the end of the season.

LONGEST WINNING STREAK—RELIEF PITCHER: 15 games, Phil Regan (Dodgers) won 13 in a row in 1966 and his first two decisions of 1967.

LONGEST LOSING STREAK: 17 games, Andy Hassler (Angels) achieved this dubious honor over two seasons, between May 4, 1975, and July 2, 1976.

Team Pitching Records, Single Game

MOST RUNS GIVEN UP, GAME: 20
The Dodgers' pitchers combined effort gave the Cubs 20 runs in Chicago May 20, 1967.

MOST RUNS GIVEN UP, INNING: 11
The Angels twice: to the Athletics, Kansas City, September 4, 1961, and to the White Sox, Chicago, May 31, 1978.

MOST HITS GIVEN UP, GAME: 26
During the 1958 season, their first in L.A., the Dodgers at the Coliseum gave 26 hits to their old crosstown rivals, the Giants, who had become cross-state rivals by moving to San Francisco the same year. The Angels since tied the record twice.

MOST CY YOUNG AWARDS: 3, Sandy Koufax, Dodgers; 1963, 1965, 1966. Only pitcher in National League to win award two years in a row.

ONLY RELIEF PITCHER TO WIN CY YOUNG AWARD: Mike Marshall, Dodgers, 1974.

Miscellaneous Team Records

LONGEST WINNING STREAK: 13 games
Dodgers twice—1962 and 1965.

LONGEST LOSING STREAK: 11 games
Angels between June 30 and July 10, 1974.
BEST DOUBLEHEADER RECORD: In 1962, the Dodgers won 7, lost 1, and split 2 twin bills.

Longest Home Game

Angels vs. Seattle Mariners, Anaheim Stadium, April 13, 1982—20 innings lasting 6 hours, 6 minutes.

Longest Away Game

Dodgers vs. Cubs, Chicago's Wrigley Field, 21 innings, lasting 6 hours, 10 minutes, August 17, 1982, Dodgers 2, Cubs 1.

Shortest Home Game

By a single minute, the Dodgers hold the record for the shortest 9-inning home game: one hour, 30 minutes against Houston Astros, May 20, 1972. Previous record: one hour, 31 minutes, Angels vs. Milwaukee Brewers.

PROFESSIONAL FOOTBALL

The Cleveland Rams became the Los Angeles Rams in 1946; the Oakland Raiders became the L.A. Raiders in 1982. These records are those set after they became Los Angeles teams.

Individual Records, Game

MOST TOUCHDOWN PASSES RECIEVED AND MOST POINTS SCORED: 4 touchdowns and 24 points, first scored by Bob Shaw (Rams) against Washington Redskins, 1949, and tied by: Elroy "Crazy Legs" Hirsch (Rams) vs. New York Yanks, 1951, Harold Jackson

(Rams) vs. Dallas Cowboys, 1973, Marcus Allen (Raiders) vs. San Diego Chargers, September 24, 1984.

MOST FIELD GOALS: 5, Bob Waterfield (Rams) vs. Detroit Lions, 1951.

LONGEST FIELD GOAL: 52 yards, kicked twice by Mike Lansford, 1985, vs. L.A. Raiders and vs. Atlanta Falcons.

MOST TOUCHDOWN PASSES: 5, first by Bob Waterfield (Rams) vs. N.Y. Bulldogs, 1949, and tied by: Norm Van Brocklin (Rams) vs. Detroit Lions, 1950; vs. N.Y. Yanks, 1951; Roman Gabriel (Rams) vs. Cleveland Browns, 1961, 1965. Vince Ferragamo (Rams) vs. New Orleans Saints 1980; S.F. 49ers, 1983.

MOST PASS COMPLETIONS: 35, Dieter Brock (Rams) in 51 attempts vs. S.F. 49ers, 1985.

MOST PASSES ATTEMPTED: 53, Jim Hardy (Rams) vs. Chicago Cardinals, 1948.

MOST YARDS GAINED PASSING: 554, Norm Van Brocklin (Rams) in 41 attempts with 27 completions vs. the N.Y. Yanks in 1951 set an N.F.L. record that still stands.

LONGEST PASSING GAIN: 96 yards, Frank Ryan (Rams) to Ollie Matson (Rams) vs. Pittsburgh Steelers, 1961.

BEST PASSING PERCENTAGE: 81.8 percent, Roman Gabriel (Rams) with 22 attempts, 18 completions vs. Baltimore Colts, 1967.

MOST PASSES INTERCEPTED: 7, Bob Waterfield (Rams) vs. Green Bay Packers in 1948.

MOST RUSHING ATTEMPTS: 36, Charles White (Rams) for a gain of 144 yards vs. Philadelphia Eagles, 1985.

MOST YARDS RUSHING: 248, Eric Dickerson (Rams) with 34 attempts and a 7.3 average vs. Dallas Cowboys, 1985. This set a play-off record. The season L.A. record is held by Willie Ellison (Rams), who gained 247 yards rushing in 26 attempts with a 9.5 average vs. New Orleans Saints 1971.

LONGEST RUN FROM SCRIMMAGE: 92 yards, Kenny Washington (Rams) vs. the Chicago Cardinals, in 1946.

MOST PASS RECEPTIONS: 18, Tom Fears (Rams) vs. Green Bay Packers, 1950, for N.F.L. record.

MOST YARDS GAINED FROM PASS RECEPTIONS: 238, Harold Jackson (Rams) vs. Dallas Cowboys in 1973.

MOST PUNT RETURNS: 9, Cle Montgomery (Raiders) vs. Detroit Lions, December 10, 1984.

MOST YARDS GAINED FROM PUNT RETURNS: 208, LeRoy Irvin (Rams) vs. Atlanta Falcons, 1981, which set the N.F.L. record. In the same game Irvin set the L.A. record and tied the N.F.L. record by scoring two touchdowns off punt returns.

LONGEST PUNT RETURN: 97 yards, Greg Pruitt (Raiders) vs. Washington Redskins, October 2, 1983.

MOST PUNTS: 12, Rusty Jackson (Rams) with a 36.1 average against the San Francisco 49ers in 1976.

BEST PUNTING AVERAGE: 52.5 yards, Danny Villanueva (Rams) 6 punts for 315 yards against San Francisco 49ers in 1962.

LONGEST PUNT: 88 yards, Bob Waterfield (Rams) vs. Green Bay Packers, 1948.

MOST POINTS AFTER TOUCHDOWN: 9, Bob Waterfield (Rams) vs. Baltimore Colts in 1950, which ties the N.F.L. record.

MOST KICKOFF RETURNS: , Drew Hill (Rams) accomplished this feat 4 times: twice in 1981 vs. New Orleans Saints and vs. Dallas Cowboys; in 1980 vs. Miami Dolphins; in 1979 vs. Cowboys. Carver Shannon (Rams) did it twice, vs. Chicago Bears, 1963, and Detroit Lions, 1964. Woodley Lewis (Rams) set the L.A. record vs. Green Bay Packers in 1953. Jim Jodat (Rams) also tied the record vs. Cleveland in 1964.

MOST YARDS GAINED BY KICKOFF RETURNS: 202, Carver Shannon (Rams) vs. Chicago Bears in 1963.

MOST TOUCHDOWNS SCORED BY KICKOFF RETURNS: 2, Ron Brown (Rams) vs. Green Bay Packers is an N.F.L. record.

LONGEST KICKOFF RETURN: 105 yards, John Arnet (Rams) vs. Detroit Lions, 1961, and tied by Travis Williams (Rams) vs. New Orleans Saints, 1971.

Top Individual Players in a Season

MOST TOUCHDOWNS SCORED: 20, Eric Dickerson (Rams), 1983.

MOST POINTS SCORED: 130, David Ray (Rams), with 30 field goals and 40 points after touchdowns, 1973.

MOST FIELD GOALS: 30, David Ray (Rams), 1973.

MOST TOUCHDOWN PASSES: 30, Vince Ferragamo (Rams), 1980.

MOST PASS COMPLETIONS AND ATTEMPTS: 274, Vince Ferragamo (Rams), with 464 attempts for a .591 percentage in 1983.

MOST YARDS GAINED PASSING: 3,276, Vince Ferragamo (Rams).

BEST PASSING PERCENTAGE: 59.7, Dieter Brock (Rams) with 365 attempts and 218 completions, 1985.

MOST PASSES INTERCEPTED BY OPPONENTS: 24, Bob Waterfield (Rams), 1949.

MOST RUSHING ATTEMPTS: 390, Eric Dickerson (Rams), 1983.

MOST YARDS GAINED RUSHING: 2,105, Eric Dickerson (Rams), 379 attempts for a 5.6 average, 1984. The yardage is an N.F.L. record.

MOST PASS RECEPTIONS: 92, Todd Christensen (Raiders), 1983.

MOST TOUCHDOWNS GAINED FROM PASS RECEPTIONS: 17, Elroy Hirsch (Rams), 1951.

MOST YARDS GAINED FROM PASS RECEPTIONS: 1,495, Elroy "Crazy Legs" Hirsch (Rams), 1951.

MOST PUNT RETURNS: 62, Fulton Walker (Raiders) in 1985.

MOST YARDS GAINED FROM PUNT RETURNS: 692, Fulton Walker (Raiders), 1985.

MOST TOUCHDOWNS SCORED FROM PUNT RETURNS: 3, LeRoy Irvin (Rams) in 1981.

MOST PUNTS: 93, Ken Clark (Rams) with a 40.1 average in 1979.

BEST PUNTING AVERAGE: 45.5, Danny Villanueva (Rams) with 87 punts in 1962.

MOST POINTS AFTER TOUCHDOWN: 54, Bob Waterfield (Rams), 1950.

MOST KICKOFF RETURNS: 60, Drew Hill (Rams), an N.F.L. record, 1981.

MOST YARDS GAINED BY KICKOFF RETURNS: 1,170, Drew Hill (Rams) in 1981.

MOST TOUCHDOWNS GAINED BY KICKOFF RETURNS: 3, V.T. Smith (Rams), 1950, and tied by Ron Brown (Rams), 1985.

Team Records, Single Game

MOST TOUCHDOWNS: 10, Rams vs. Baltimore Colts, 1950, ties the N.F.L. record.

MOST TOUCHDOWNS, RUSHING: 7, Rams vs. Atlanta Falcons, 1976.

MOST TOUCHDOWNS, PASSING: 6, Rams twice in 1949 against New York Bulldogs and Washington Redskins and in 1950 vs. Detroit Lions.

MOST FIELD GOALS: 5, Rams vs. Detroit Lions, 1951.

MOST POINTS: 70, Rams, who in 1950 whomped the Baltimore Colts 70 to 17. Surprisingly this set no league records.

MOST TOTAL YARDS GAINED: 735, Rams vs. the New York Yanks, 1951, an N.F.L. record.

MOST PASS COMPLETIONS: 35, Rams vs. San Francisco 49ers in 1985.

MOST PASSES ATTEMPTED: 55, Rams vs. Philadelphia Eagles, 1950.

MOST YARDS GAINED PASSING: 554, Rams vs. New York Yanks for the N.F.L. record.

MOST RUSHING ATTEMPTS: 65, Rams vs. Minnesota Vikings, 1976.

MOST YARDS GAINED RUSHING: 371, Rams vs. N.Y. Yanks, 1951.

MOST FIRST DOWNS: 38, Rams vs. New York Giants, 1966, an N.F.L. record.

MOST FIRST DOWNS, PASSING: 21, by the Rams vs. New York Yanks, 1951; Pittsburgh Steelers, 1952; Chicago Bears, 1982.

MOST FIRST DOWNS, RUSHING: 21, Rams vs. New Orleans Saints, 1973.

MOST YARDS GAINED, PUNT RETURNS: 219, Rams vs. Atlanta Falcons, 1981.

MOST PUNTS: 12, Rams vs. San Francisco 49ers, 1976.

MOST SAFETIES: 3, Rams in third quarter vs. N.Y. Giants, 1984; an N.F.L. record.

Team Records for a Single Season

MOST VICTORIES: 12, Rams in 1973, 1975, and 1978.

MOST CONSECUTIVE VICTORIES: 14, Rams in 1967–68 season.

L. A. SUPERLATIVES

MOST TOUCHDOWNS: 64, Rams, 1950.
MOST TOUCHDOWNS, RUSHING: 33, Rams, 1950.
MOST TOUCHDOWNS, PASSING: 31, Rams, 1950 and 1980.
MOST FIELD GOALS: 30, Rams, 1973.
MOST POINTS SCORED: 466, Rams, 1950.
MOST POINTS ALLOWED: 353, Rams, 1950.
FEWEST POINTS ALLOWED: 135, Rams, 1975.
MOST TOTAL YARDS GAINED: 6,006, Rams, 1980.
MOST PASS COMPLETIONS: 286, Rams, 1983.
MOST PASSES ATTEMPTED: 489, Rams, 1983.
MOST YARDS GAINED PASSING: 3,910, Raiders, 1983.
BEST PASSING PERCENTAGE: 58.5, Rams, 1983.
MOST PASSES INTERCEPTED: 38, Rams, 1952.
MOST YARDS RETURNING INTERCEPTIONS: 712, Rams, 1952.
MOST PASSES INTERCEPTED BY OPPONENTS: 32, Rams, 1981.
MOST RUSHING ATTEMPTS: 659, Rams, 1973.
MOST YARDS GAINED RUSHING: 2,925, Rams, 1973.
MOST FIRST DOWNS: 356, Raiders, 1983.
MOST FIRST DOWNS PASSING: 157, Rams, 1980.
MOST FIRST DOWNS RUSHING: 177, Rams, 1973.
MOST FIRST DOWNS, PENALTIES: 32, Raiders, 1983.
MOST PUNT RETURNS: 71, Raiders, 1985.
MOST YARDS GAINED FROM PUNT RETURNS: 792, Raiders, 1985.
MOST PUNTS: 95, Rams, 1979.
BEST PUNTING AVERAGE: 45.5 yards, Rams, 1962.
MOST KICKOFF RETURNS: 70, Rams, 1963.
MOST YARDS GAINED BY KICKOFF RETURNS: 1,651, Rams, 1963.
MOST TOUCHDOWNS GAINED BY KICKOFF RETURNS: 3, Rams, 1950 and 1985.

MOST FUMBLES: 46, Raiders, 1983.
MOST PENALTIES: 143, Raiders, 1984.
MOST YARDS PENALIZED: 1,169, Rams, 1978.

PROFESSIONAL BASKETBALL

Professional basketball first bounced into Los Angeles in 1960 when the Lakers moved from their Minneapolis birthplace to hold court as the Los Angeles Lakers in the newly built Los Angeles Sports Arena, basketball capacity 15,371 seats. On December 31, 1967, they played and won their first game in their present home, the Forum, with a basketball capacity of 17,505.

L.A. adopted its second N.B.A. basketball team as the whistle blew to signal the start of the 1984–85 season. The San Diego Clippers had moved north to the Sports Arena and become the Los Angeles Clippers.

All-Time Leaders

Kareem Abdul-Jabbar, who began his pro basketball career with the Lakers in 1969 and is playing for them still today, holds probably more all-time N.B.A. records than any player ever to wear an L.A. uniform.

MOST POINTS SCORED, REGULAR SEASON: 35,108.
MOST POINTS SCORED, PLAY-OFFS: 4,912.
MOST MINUTES PLAYED: 51,002.
MOST GAMES PLAYED, REGULAR SEASON: 1,328.
MOST GAMES PLAYED, PLAY-OFFS: 180.
MOST FIELD GOALS ATTEMPTED: 25,752.
MOST BLOCKED SHOTS: 2,915.

MOST MVP AWARDS: 6, for the 1971, 1972, 1974, 1976, 1977, and 1979 seasons.

Top Player Individual Performances in a Single Game

MOST POINTS SCORED: 71, Elgin Baylor (Lakers) vs. New York Knicks on November 15, 1960. In that game he also set the L.A. record for scoring the most points in a half with 37 and also in a quarter with 24. Jerry West (Lakers) also racked up 24 points in one quarter, also against the Knicks on January 17, 1962.

MOST FIELD GOALS MADE: 29, Wilt Chamberlain (Lakers), vs. Phoenix Suns on February 9, 1969.

MOST FIELD GOALS ATTEMPTED: 55, Elgin Baylor (Lakers), vs. Philadelphia 76ers on December 2, 1961.

MOST FIELD GOALS ATTEMPTED (IN A HALF): 28, Elgin Baylor (Lakers), vs. New York Knicks on November 15, 1960. In that same game he also set the L.A. record for most FTAs in a quarter with 18.

MOST FREE THROWS MADE: 20, Jerry West (Lakers) tied the L.A. record three times: vs. San Francisco on December 21, 1962, and again on February 21, 1966, and vs. New York Knicks on January 8, 1966. Elgin Baylor (Lakers) originally set the record against St. Louis on December 21, 1962.

MOST FREE THROW ATTEMPTS: 30, Wilt Chamberlain (Lakers), vs. Philadelphia 76ers on October 17, 1969.

MOST FREE THROW ATTEMPTS (IN A HALF): 15, Jerry West (Lakers), vs. New York Knicks on October 22, 1963.

MOST TOTAL REBOUNDS: 42, Wilt Chamberlain (Lakers), vs. Boston Celtics on March 7, 1969.

MOST TOTAL REBOUNDS (IN A HALF): 27, Wilt Chamberlain (Lakers), vs. Boston Celtics on March 7, 1969.

MOST TOTAL REBOUNDS (IN A QUARTER): 14, an L.A. record set by Gene Wiley (Lakers) vs. New York Knicks on November 5, 1962, and then tied by Harold "Happy" Hairston vs. Philadelphia 76ers on November 15, 1974.

MOST OFFENSIVE REBOUNDS: 13, Earvin "Magic" Johnson (Lakers), vs. Houston Rockets on March 21, 1982.

MOST DEFENSIVE REBOUNDS: 29, Kareem Abdul-Jabbar (Lakers), vs. Detroit Pistons on December 14, 1975.

MOST ASSISTS: 23, Jerry West (Lakers) set the L.A. record vs. Philadelphia 76ers on February 1, 1967, and it was tied by Earvin Johnson (Lakers), vs. Seattle Supersonics on February 21, 1984. In that same game Johnson also set the L.A. record for most assists in one half with 18.

MOST STEALS: 10, Jerry West (Lakers), vs. Seattle Supersonics on December 17, 1973.

MOST BLOCKED SHOTS: 17, Elmore Smith (Lakers), vs. Portland Trail Blazers on October 28, 1973.

Top Individual Player Performances, Season

MOST POINTS SCORED: 2,719, Elgin Baylor (Lakers), 1962–63.

HIGHEST SCORING AVERAGE: 38.3, Elgin Baylor (Lakers), 1961–62.

HIGHEST FIELD GOAL PERCENTAGE: .727, Wilt Chamberlain (Lakers), which led the N.B.A. in the 1972–73 season.

MOST FIELD GOALS MADE: 1,029, Elgin Baylor (Lakers), 1962–63.

MOST FIELD GOALS ATTEMPTED: 2,273, Elgin Baylor (Lakers), 1962–63.

MOST FREE THROWS MADE: 840, Jerry West (Lakers), 1965–66.

MOST FREE THROWS ATTEMPTED: 977, Jerry West (Lakers), 1965–66.

HIGHEST FREE THROW PERCENTAGE: .892, Cazzie Russell (Lakers), 1975–76.

MOST TOTAL REBOUNDS: 1,712, Wilt Chamberlain (Lakers), which led the N.B.A. in the 1968–69 season.

MOST OFFENSIVE REBOUNDS: 335, Harold "Happy" Hairston (Lakers), 1973–74.

MOST DEFENSIVE REBOUNDS: 1,111, Kareem Abdul-Jabbar (Lakers), 1975–76.

MOST STEALS: 208, Earvin Johnson (Lakers), 1981–82.

MOST ASSISTS: 968, Earvin Johnson (Lakers), 1984–85.

MOST BLOCKED SHOTS: 393, Elmore Smith (Lakers), which led the N.B.A. in the 1973–74 season.

Most Minutes Played in a Single Season

Wilt Chamberlain of the Lakers set not only a Los Angeles record, but also an N.B.A. record by playing 3,669 minutes during the 1968–69 season.

Top Team Performances in a Game

MOST POINTS: 162, Lakers vs. Golden State Warriors on March 19, 1972. In that same game the Lakers set the L.A. record for most field goals made with 69.

MOST POINTS (IN A HALF): 91, Lakers had L.A. record halfs twice—vs. Chicago Bulls on January 23, 1966, and again vs. Golden State Warriors on March 19, 1972.

MOST FIELD GOALS MADE: 69, Lakers vs. Golden State Warriors on March 19, 1972.

MOST TOTAL REBOUNDS: 75, Lakers vs. Seattle Supersonics on February 15, 1974.

MOST ASSISTS: 51, Lakers vs. Denver Nuggets on February 23, 1982.

MOST STEALS: 23, Lakers vs. Kansas City on November 9, 1982.

Top Team Performances, Season

MOST WINS: 69, Lakers, 1971–72.

MOST HOME WINS: 37, Lakers, in 1976–77 and again in 1979–80.

MOST AWAY WINS: 31, Lakers, 1971–72.

MOST POINTS: 9,937, Lakers, 1967–68.

HIGHEST SCORING AVERAGE: 121.2, Lakers, 1967–68.

MOST FIELD GOALS MADE: 3,964, Lakers, 1982–83.

MOST FIELD GOALS ATTEMPTED: 8,466, Lakers, 1966–67.

HIGHEST FIELD GOAL PERCENTAGE: .545, Lakers, 1984–85.

HIGHEST 3-POINT FIELD GOAL PERCENTAGE: .337, Lakers, 1985–86.

MOST FREE THROWS MADE: 2,378, Lakers, 1961–62.

MOST FREE THROW ATTEMPTS: 3,240, Lakers, 1961–62.

MOST TOTAL REBOUNDS: 5,816, Lakers, 1960–61.

MOST BLOCKED SHOTS: 653, Lakers, 1973–74.

MOST ASSISTS: 2,575, Lakers, 1984–85.

MOST TURNOVERS: 1,913, Lakers, 1973–74.

Longest Winning Streak

On their way to the 1971–72 N.B.A. championship, the

L. A. SUPERLATIVES   227

Lakers racked up 33 consecutive wins, an L.A. professional basketball record. The Lakers' streak began with a win against Baltimore on November 5, 1971, and was ended by the Milwaukee Bucks on January 9, 1972.

COLLEGE SPORTS

The varsities of the UCLA Bruins and the USC Trojans, both members of the Pac Ten League, dominate collegiate sports in the L.A. area. For this first edition, we are considering only the records set by these two universities. However, we will be glad to hear from other collegiate athletes whose records may surpass those of USC and UCLA and include them in subsequent editions.

MOST WINNING VOLLEYBALL COACH

Al Scales of UCLA has more wins to his credit than any other volleyball coach in Los Angeles or in college volleyball anywhere.

MOST MEN'S NCAA TEAM CHAMPIONSHIPS

USC men's varsity teams lead not only the L.A. area collegiate teams but also hold a record of 63 NCAA titles in sports that include basketball, football, tennis, volleyball, gymnastics, soccer, track and field, swimming, and water polo.

MOST WOMEN'S NCAA CHAMPIONSHIPS

The women's softball, track and field, and volleyball teams of UCLA have chalked up a total of 3 NCAA titles to make them the winningest female varsity teams in the nation. They also hold AIAW national championships in volleyball, track and field, softball, basketball, and tennis.

MOST TENNIS CHAMPIONSHIPS

With a record 15 NCAA championships in tennis, the UCLA Bruins hold more titles in this sport than any other school in the nation.

COLLEGE FOOTBALL

Most Heisman Trophy Winners

The University of Southern California leads all colleges in the Greater Los Angeles area in the number of Heisman Trophy winners for football, with four since 1965: 1965, Mike Garrett; 1968, O. J. Simpson; 1979, Charles White; 1981, Marcus Allen. UCLA had one—Gary Beban in 1967.

Top Performance By An Individual Player, Game

MOST POINTS AND TOUCHDOWNS: Anthony Davis (USC), tied two Pac-10 records when he scored 36 points and 6 touchdowns against Notre Dame in 1972.

MOST FIELD GOALS MADE: 6, John Lee (UCLA), vs. San Diego State in 1984.

LONGEST FIELD GOAL: 55 yards, Frank Corral (UCLA), vs. Oregon in 1976.

MOST YARDS GAINED PASSING: 399, Steve Bono (UCLA), vs. BYU in 1983.

MOST PASS COMPLETIONS: 29, Tom Ramsey (UCLA), vs. Arizona in 1982.

LONGEST PASS PLAY: 93 yards, Mike Frankovich (UCLA) to Ransom Linvesay vs. Oregon in 1932.

MOST PASSES ATTEMPTED: 51, Dennis Dummit (UCLA), vs. California in 1970.

MOST TOUCHDOWN RECEPTIONS: 4, Jojo Townsell (UCLA), vs. Long Beach State in 1982.

MOST PASS RECEPTIONS: 11, Rick Wilkes (UCLA), vs. USC in 1970, and tied by Fred Hill (USC) vs. Washington State in 1964, and Jeff Simmons (USC) in 1982 against both Arizona State and Notre Dame.

MOST YARDS ON PASS RECEPTIONS: 201, Hal Bedsole (USC), vs. California in 1962.

MOST YARDS RUSHING: 347, Ricky Bell (USC), vs. Washington State.

TOTAL YARDS GAINED: 400, Steve Bono (UCLA), vs. BYU in 1983.

MOST PASS INTERCEPTIONS: 4, Adrian Young (USC), vs. Notre Dame in 1972, ties a Pac-10 record.

HIGHEST AVERAGE GAIN PER KICKOFF RETURN: 72.7, by Anthony Davis (USC) with 3 for 218 yards vs. Notre Dame in 1972, is an NCAA record.

LONGEST PUNT RETURN: 94 yards, Kermit Alexander (UCLA), vs. Stanford in 1961.

Top Performance by a Player, Season

MOST POINTS SCORED: 138, Marcus Allen (USC), 1981.

MOST TOUCHDOWNS SCORED: 23, Marcus Allen (USC), 1981.

MOST PASS COMPLETIONS: 209, Tom Ramsey (UCLA), 1982.

MOST PASSING ATTEMPTS: 344, Dennis Dummit (UCLA), 1970.

HIGHEST COMPLETION PERCENTAGE: 69.3, Rick Neuheisel (UCLA), 1983.

MOST PASSES HAD INTERCEPTED: 19, Dennis Dummit (UCLA), 1970.

LOWEST RATE OF INTERCEPTIONS: 2.1 percent, Paul McDonald (USC), 1979.

MOST YARD GAINED PASSING: 2,986, Tom Ramsey (UCLA), 1982.

MOST TOUCHDOWN PASSES: 21, Tom Ramsey (UCLA), 1982.

MOST EXTRA KICK POINTS SCORED: 117, John Lee (UCLA), 1984.

MOST FIELD GOALS MADE: 32, John Lee (UCLA), 1984.

MOST PUNT RETURNS: 47, Mike Battle (USC), 1967.

MOST YARDS GAINED ON PUNT RETURNS: 570, Mike Battle (USC), 1967.

HIGHEST RUSHING AVERAGE: 12.2, Jackie Robinson (UCLA), 1939.

Rushing

Marcus Allen of USC holds possibly more NCAA regular-season rushing records than any single L.A.–area collegiate player for his efforts in the 1981 season:

MOST TIMES CARRIED BALL: 403.

MOST YARDS GAINED RUSHING: 2,342.

HIGHEST PER GAME RUSHING AVERAGE: 212.9.

MOST ALL-PURPOSE RUSHING PLAYS: 432.

MOST YARDS GAINED ALL-PURPOSE RUSHING: 2,559.

Biggest Football Score

Whittier College set an area record when they racked up 103 points against the Bruins in 1920.

Largest Shutout

The greatest point disparity in a shutout occurred in 1925 when USC beat Pomona 80–0.

Lowest Score

The lowest score by which a collegiate football game has been won in the L.A. area was racked up by USC vs. the 211th Infantry in 1917. The score: Trojans 3, Infantry 0.

Best Team Performance, Game

MOST TOUCHDOWNS: 12, USC vs. Cal Tech in 1924; Pomona, 1925; Arizona, 1928; and UCLA, 1929.

MOST YARDS GAINED, TOTAL OFFENSE: 978, USC vs. Pomona in 1925.

FEWEST YARDS, TOTAL OFFENSE: 41, UCLA vs. Syracuse in 1964.

MOST YARDS GAINED RUSHING: 753, USC vs. UCLA in 1929.

FEWEST YARDS GAINED: −37, UCLA vs. Syracuse in 1964.

MOST YARDS GAINED PASSING: 399, UCLA vs. BYU in 1983.

MOST PASS COMPLETIONS: 29, UCLA vs. Arizona in 1982.

MOST PASS ATTEMPTS: 51, UCLA vs. California in 1970.

FEWEST PASS ATTEMPTS: 0, USC vs. College of the Pacific, 1945.

MOST FIRST DOWNS: 43, USC vs. Pomona, 1925.

MOST FIELD GOALS: 6, UCLA vs. San Diego State, 1984.

Top Team Performances, Season

MOST POINTS SCORED: 492, USC, 1929.
FEWEST POINTS SCORED: 59, UCLA, 1943.
MOST TOUCHDOWNS: 75, USC, 1929.
FEWEST TOUCHDOWNS: 64, UCLA, 1943.
MOST FIELD GOALS: 32, UCLA, 1984.
MOST EXTRA POINTS: 60, UCLA, 1973.
MOST YARDS GAINED RUSHING: 4,403, UCLA, 1973.
MOST YARDS GAINED PASSING: 3,232, UCLA, 1982.
MOST YARDS, TOTAL OFFENSE: 5,655, USC, 1979.
FEWEST YARDS, TOTAL OFFENSE: 1,290, UCLA, 1943.
MOST PASSES COMPLETED: 223, UCLA, 1982.
MOST TOUCHDOWN PASSES: 23, UCLA, 1982.
FEWEST TOUCHDOWN PASSES: 1, USC, 1946.
MOST INTERCEPTIONS: 34, UCLA, 1952.
MOST CONSECUTIVE GAMES WITHOUT A DEFEAT: 28, USC, 1978 to 1980.
MOST CONSECUTIVE GAMES WITHOUT BEING SHUT OUT: USC holds not only the L.A. but also the NCAA record of 186 games, from 1967 to 1983.
MOST CONSECUTIVE GAMES SCORED IN: 169, by UCLA from 1971 to 1985, is the longest current streak in the NCAA and the third longest in history.

COLLEGE BASKETBALL

Largest College Basketball Crowd

The USC–UCLA game at the Sports Arena, March 9, 1974, drew the largest crowd ever to attend a college basketball game in Los Angeles, 15,387.

Most Straight Wins in Basketball History

The college basketball team that scored the most consecutive wins in history was the UCLA Bruins, who won 88 straight games between 1971 and 1974.

Top Performance Individual Player, Game

MOST POINTS: 87, Lew Alcindor* (UCLA), vs. Washington State in 1967.

MOST REBOUNDS: 28, Willie Naulls (UCLA) vs. Arizona State in 1956 and tied by Cliff Robinson (USC), vs. Portland State in 1978.

MOST FIELD GOALS: 26, Lew Alcindor* (UCLA), vs. Washington State in 1967.

Top Individual Performances, Season

MOST POINTS: 870, Lew Alcindor* (UCLA), 1967.

HIGHEST SCORING AVERAGE: 29.0, Lew Alcindor* (UCLA), 1967.

MOST REBOUNDS: 506, Bill Walton (UCLA), 1973.

HIGHEST REBOUNDING AVERAGE: 16.9, Bill Walton (UCLA), 1973.

MOST FIELD GOALS: 364, Lew Alcindor* (UCLA), 1967.

MOST FIELD GOAL ATTEMPTS: 582, Willie Naulls (UCLA), 1956.

HIGHEST FIELD GOAL PERCENTAGE: 66.7, Lew Alcindor* (UCLA), 1967.

MOST FREE THROWS: 202, Reggie Miller (UCLA), 1986.

---

* College star Lew Alcindor went on to achieve superstardom in the N.B.A. as Kareem Abdul-Jabbar.

HIGHEST FREE THROW PERCENTAGE: 95.0, Rod Foster (UCLA), 1982.
MOST ASSISTS: 201, Roy Hamilton (UCLA), 1979.
MOST STEALS: 53, Roy Hamilton (UCLA), 1979.
MOST CONSECUTIVE FREE THROWS: 37, John Block (USC) in three games in 1966.

Top Team Performances, Game

MOST POINTS: 133, UCLA vs. Louisiana State, 1969.
MOST POINTS IN A UCLA VS. USC GAME: 107, by UCLA in 1967.
MOST FREE THROWS MADE: 47, UCLA vs. USC, 1956.
MOST FREE THROW ATTEMPTS: 63, UCLA vs. USC, 1956.

Top Team Performances, Season

MOST POINTS: 2,838, UCLA, 1972.
HIGHEST SCORING AVERAGE: 94.6, UCLA, 1972.
MOST REBOUNDS: 1,670, UCLA, 1964.
HIGHEST REBOUNDING AVERAGE: 55.7, UCLA, 1964.
MOST FIELD GOALS: 1,161, UCLA, 1968.
MOST FIELD GOAL ATTEMPTS: 2,333, UCLA, 1950.
HIGHEST FIELD GOAL AVERAGE: 55.5, UCLA, 1979.
MOST FREE THROWS: 642, UCLA, 1956.
MOST FIELD GOALS ATTEMPTED: 967, USC, 1957.
MOST VICTORIES: 30, UCLA in 1964, 1967, 1972, and 1973.
BEST RECORD: 30 wins, no losses, UCLA, in 1964, 1967, 1972, and 1973.

HIGH SCHOOL RECORDS

Boys Track and Field

100-METER DASH: 10.44, Henry Thomas (Hawthorne), 1984.

200-METER DASH: 20.77, Henry Thomas (Hawthorne), 1984.

400-METER DASH: 45.7, Chip Rish (Marina-Huntington Beach), 1985.

800-METER RUN: 1:50.55, Chauncy Isom (Westchester), 1982.

1,600-METER RUN: 4:05.4, Mark Schilling (Garden Grove), 1972.

3,200-METER RUN: 9:06.4, Jose Amaya (Wilson), 1971.

4 × 100 RELAY: 41.13, Taft, in 1986.

4 × 400 RELAY: 3:12.74, Fremont, in 1984.

100-METER HURDLES: 13.74, Phillip Johnson (Gardena), 1978.

300-METER HURDLES: 37.08, Anthony Reynolds (Fremont), 1984.

HIGH JUMP: 7 foot-3¼ inches, Lee Balkin (Glendale), 1979.

LONG JUMP: 24 foot-3¼ inches, Larry Nelson (Simi Valley), 1985.

TRIPLE JUMP: 49 foot-2¼ inches, Cary Tyler (Washington), 1977.

POLE VAULT: 17 feet-½ inch, Anthony Curran (Crespi), 1978.

SHOT PUT: 64 feet-8¾ inch, Dave Gerasimchuk (Narbonne), 1972.

Girls Track and Field

100-METER DASH: 11.58, Tesha Giddens (Locke), 1985.

200-METER DASH: 23.19, Sheri Howard (Kennedy), 1980.

400-METER DASH: 52.39, Denean Howard (Kennedy), 1982.

800-METER RUN: 2:04.91, Trena Hall (Compton), 1984.

1,600-METER RUN: 4:39.92, Polly Anne Plumer (Irvine), 1982.

4 × 100 RELAY: 45.50, Dorsey, in 1982.

4 × 400 RELAY: 3:39.62, Kennedy, in 1980.

100-METER HURDLES: 13.78, Chewaukii Knighten (Locke), 1985.

300-METER HURDLES: 42.70, Millisa King (Fremont), 1984.

HIGH JUMP: 5 foot-8½ inches, Linda Soja (Polytechnic), 1980.

LONG JUMP: 19 foot-10¼ inches, Gwen Loud (Westchester), 1979.

SHOT PUT: 53 foot-7½ inches, Natalie Kaaiawahia (Fullerton), 1983.

Boys Swimming

50-YARD FREESTYLE: 21.27, Bob Balducchi (El Camino Real), 1985.

100-YARD FREESTYLE: 45.83, Bob Balducchi (El Camino Real), 1985.

200-YARD FREESTYLE: 1:39.47, Brian Roney (El Camino Real), 1978.

500-YARD FREESTYLE: 4:25.05, Brian Roney (El Camino Real), 1978.

200-YARD INDIVIDUAL MEDLEY: 1:55.22, Jeff Klein (Kennedy), 1982.

100-YARD BUTTERFLY: 50.77, Tom Liliekis (El Camino Real), 1984.

100-YARD BACKSTROKE: 51.64, Franz Szymanski (Palisades), 1976.

100-YARD BREASTSTROKE: 58.22, Eric Wennerstrom (Chatsworth), 1980.

200-YARD MEDLEY RELAY: 1:38.91, Palisades, 1975.

400-YARD FREESTYLE RELAY: 3:10.87, El Camino Real, 1984.

Girls Swimming

50-YARD FREESTYLE: 24.70, Stephanie Hoisch (Reseda), 1985.

100-YARD FREESTYLE: 53.17, Tana Vandeweghe (Palisades), 1976.

200-YARD FREESTYLE: 1:55.04, Melissa Rossie (El Camino Real) 1979.

500-YARD FREESTYLE: 5:01.94, Melissa Rossie (El Camino Real), 1979.

200-YARD INDEPENDENT MEDLEY: 2:11.42, Michele Saxer (Palisades), 1986.

100-YARD BUTTERFLY: 58.78, Kim Schlegal (Palisades), 1981.

100-YARD BACKSTROKE: 59.60, Kim Schlegal (Palisades), 1981.

100-YARD BREASTSTROKE: 1:09.42, Morgan Brown (Venice), 1982.

200-YARD MEDLEY RELAY: 1:55.86, Palisades, 1985.

400-YARD FREESTYLE RELAY: 3:43.66, El Camino Real, 1985.

Football: Longest Interception Return

James Washington set an L.A. city record with his 95-yard interception return when he was playing for Jordan High.

Top Area High School Football Team

Pasadena High set a California Interscholastic Federation

record when it won its 12th straight league football title in 1982.

Top L.A. City High School Football Team

Manual Arts High School holds the record for the best all-time city high school football team by winning 15 championships and trying for three since 1913.

Boys High School Best All-Time Record

Crenshaw High School is not only the all-time top city high school basketball team, having won L.A. championships three times and trying six times, but the school has gone on to win the state basketball California Interscholastic Foundation title twice.

Top Performances In City Boys School Basketball Championships, Individual Player

MOST POINTS, FORWARD, GAME: 44, Dwayne Polee (Manual Arts), 1981, tied by John Williams (Crenshaw) in 1984. In 1981 Polee also set the scoring records for an individual in a half with 29 and for a quarter with 18 points.

MOST POINTS, FORWARD, TOURNAMENT: 148, Dwayne Polee (Manual Arts), 1981.

MOST POINTS, CENTER, GAME: 46, Curtis Rowe (Fremont), 1967.

MOST POINTS, CENTER, TOURNAMENT: 135, Chet Noe (Washington), 1949.

MOST POINTS, GUARD, GAME: 42, Wilbert Williams (Jefferson), 1976.

MOST POINTS, GUARD, TOURNAMENT: 212, Tony Horton (University), 1962.

Boys Basketball Team Performances

MOST POINTS, GAME: 126, Jefferson vs. Huntington Park, tied by Crenshaw when they beat Roosevelt in 1973.

MOST POINTS, TOURNAMENT: 417, Jefferson, 1966.

MOST POINTS, ONE HALF: 69, Crenshaw set the record vs. Roosevelt in 1973 and tied it against Huntington Park in 1976.

MOST POINTS, ONE QUARTER: 44, Jefferson vs. Huntington Park, 1966.

Top Team Performances In State CIF* Championships

MOST POINTS SCORED, GAME: 72, Crenshaw, 1985.

MOST FIELD GOALS MADE: 32, Banning, 1982.

MOST FREE THROWS ATTEMPTED: 32, Crenshaw, 1985.

MOST REBOUNDS: 42, Crenshaw, 1985.

MOST ASSISTS: 20, Carson, 1982.

Girls High School Basketball City Champ

Locke High's girls basketball team holds the L.A. record for most city championships with two titles and three ties. The school also owns the city's only CIF* state championship trophy by winning that tournament in 1981.

Girls High School Basketball State Champ

Only one Southern California girls high school basketball team, Buena High in Ventura, has won two state championships in CIF* tournament play.

*California Interscholastic Federation

Girls High School Basketball Top Player Performances, CIF State Tourneys

MOST POINTS SCORED: 41, Cheryl Miller (Polytechnic, Riverside), 1982.

MOST FIELD GOALS MADE: 19, Cheryl Miller (Polytechnic, Riverside), 1982.

MOST FREE THROWS MADE: 10, Cheryl Nelson (Marshall Fundamental, Pasadena), 1983.

MOST FREE THROWS ATTEMPTED: 13, Cynthia Cooper (Locke), 1981, which was tied by Cheryl Nelson (Marshall Fundamental, Pasadena) 1983.

MOST REBOUNDS: 20, Taja Winston (Locke), 1981.

MOST ASSISTS: 13, Renee Overton (Polytechnic, Riverside).

Girls High School Basketball Top Team Performances, CIF Tourney Play

MOST POINTS SCORED: 77, Polytechnic, Riverside, 1982.

MOST FIELD GOALS MADE: 36, Polytechnic, Riverside, 1982.

MOST FREE THROWS MADE: 19, Locke, 1981.

MOST FREE THROWS ATTEMPTED: 36, Locke, 1981.

MOST REBOUNDS: 51, Locke, 1981.

MOST ASSISTS: 18, Buena, Ventura, 1983.

Fun & Games from WARNER BOOKS

__ **THE COMPLETE UNABRIDGED SUPER TRIVIA
ENCYCLOPEDIA** (V32-378, $4.95, U.S.A.)
by Fred L. Worth (V32-379, $5.95, Canada)

Xavier Cugat's theme song? The bestseller of 1929? Miss Hungary of 1936? Here's more than 800 pages of pure entertainment for collectors, gamblers, crossword puzzle addicts and those who want to stroll down memory lane. It asks every question, answers it correctly, solves every argument.

__ **THE COMPLETE UNABRIDGED SUPER TRIVIA
ENCYCLOPEDIA, Volume II** (V32-622, $4.95, U.S.A.)
by Fred L. Worth (V32-623, $5.95, Canada)

Okay, wise guy . . . so you think you know trivia, do you? Well, do you know which well-known TV actor directed the movie BEWARE! The BLOB? Sarah Barney Belcher's genealogical claim to fame? Muhammad Ali's aptly chosen CB handle? The presidential owner of Beans, the Boston bulldog? Which famous multimillionaire went down with the *Titanic*?

__ **BOXED SET OF THE COMPLETE
UNABRIDGED SUPER TRIVIA** (V11-241, $9.90, U.S.A.)
ENCYCLOPEDIA, Vols. I & II (V11-242, $11.90, Canada)

__ **THE COMPLETE UNABRIDGED SUPER** (V32-164, $4.95, U.S.A.)
TRIVIA ENCYCLOPEDIA, Volume III (V32-165, $5.95, Canada)

Who was the first woman admitted into the Hall of Fame for Famous Legs? What states meet at Four Corners, U.S.A.? Which baseball player has the lifetime record for most errors? . . . This is Fred Worth's latest compilation of all categories of trivia, from sports to television, films to rock groups, celebrity sayings to obscure statistics, geography, politics, and much more.

WARNER BOOKS
P.O. Box 690
New York, N.Y. 10019

Please send me the books I have checked. I enclose a check or money order (not cash), plus 50¢ per order and 50¢ per copy to cover postage and handling.*
(Allow 4 weeks for delivery.)

_____ Please send me your free mail order catalog. (If ordering only the catalog, include a large self-addressed, stamped envelope.)

Name _____

Address _____

City _____

State _____ Zip _____

*N.Y. State and California residents add applicable sales tax. 100

TEST YOUR INTELLIGENCE

__ **GAMES FOR THE**
SUPERINTELLIGENT (V31-421, $3.50, U.S.A.)
by James F. Fixx (V31-420, $4.50, Canada)

Are you superintelligent? This book can help you find out. But even if it doesn't, it will provide hours of mind-expanding entertainment guaranteed to inflate your ego—or drive you quite crazy.

__ **MORE GAMES FOR**
THE SUPERINTELLIGENT (V31-347, $2.95, U.S.A.)
by James F. Fixx (V31-348, $3.75, Canada)

Test your mind. Learn how to improve your thinking. And have wonderful fun doing it! Your intelligence is meant to be used—and this is the book that lets you put it into play in mind games that prove what a pleasure puzzles can be.

__ **SOLVE IT** (V31-080, $2.95, U.S.A.)
by James F. Fixx (V31-081, $3.75, Canada)

Word, number, and design puzzles to bring every aspect of your mental powers into play.

__ **THE NEW YORK TIMES CROSSWORD**
PUZZLE DICTIONARY
by Thomas Pulliam & (V38-250, $12.50, U.S.A.)
Clare Grundman (V38-251, $16.95, Canada)

Indispensable for all real crossword puzzle fans. It's the largest collection of synonyms ever published—more than half a million words in four thousand entries, arranged alphabetically by word length. And the thousands of geographical and foreign answer words are listed in special designed "shaded" boxes for easy location. An over-sized paperback.

WARNER BOOKS
P.O. Box 690
New York, N.Y. 10019

Please send me the books I have checked. I enclose a check or money order (not cash), plus 50¢ per order and 50¢ per copy to cover postage and handling.*
(Allow 4 weeks for delivery.)

_____ Please send me your free mail order catalog. (If ordering only the catalog, include a large self-addressed, stamped envelope.)

Name _____

Address _____

City _____

State _____ Zip _____

*N.Y. State and California residents add applicable sales tax.